CREATIVE DIVINATION
Read Tea Leaves & Develop
Your Personal Code

Tabitha Dial

Dial, Tabitha

Creative Divination: Read Tea Leaves & Develop Your Personal Code by Tabitha Dial

ISBN-13: 978-1986827898
ISBN-10: 1986827895

1. Divination > General
2. Tasseomancy
3. Self-Help

For inquiries about volume orders, please contact:
tabithadial@gmail.com

Tabitha Dial
North Star Muse
www.northstarmuse.com

Published in the United States by CreateSpace
Distributed by Tabitha Dial
Cover & Interior by Ana Maria Selvaggio | Renmeleon.com

10 9 8 7 6 5 4 3 2 1
Printed in the United States of America

What people are saying about *Creative Divination*:

Curious humans! Here we are, in physical form on this amazing earth, looking around and within ourselves in every way imaginable, trying to better understand how to navigate our lives. For thousands of years, we've tracked the motion of planets and stars; thrown the bones, the shells, the runes, the cards; scryed with flames or crystals or mirrors; sought clues in the shape of clouds and the flight of birds...

Of all the oracular avenues available to us, tea leaf reading is one of the most satisfying. First, of course, there's a cup of tea! And then, in the damp leaves left behind, images reveal themselves. And brava, Tabitha Dial! Rather than offer a list of symbols with static meanings to be memorized, Dial refers us back to our own intuitions and interpretations. This emphasis on personal meaning shifts us from head to heart, and brings us clearly into the authentic spirit of true oracle work.

Of equal importance, Dial focuses in on a vital divinatory point that too often gets glossed over: How to frame our questions. Remember, a simple "yes-no" query yields the least information. Instead, in almost 80 practice readings, dial steps us through themes and nuances, framing aspects of each type of question in ways that can deliver a wealth of information, which in turn allows us to make our own better-informed decisions.

Tabitha Dial's wise exploratory and intuitive approach makes tea leaf reading – this delicious but mysterious form of divination – far more accessible to all seekers.

- Renna Shesso, author of *Math for Mystics*

In her new book, Creative Divination: Read Tea Leaves and Develop Your Personal Code, *Tabitha Dial gives us a delightful introduction and informative guide to the art of reading tea leaves, or tasseomancy in divination parlance. Her guide is wispy on woo-woo and meaty on metaphysical psychology, the way in which we experience unseen realities. Those interested in exploring the art and science of divination – any type of divination – will find this offering both unique and invaluable. Included are useful tips on how* to read tea leaves from a beginner's perspective along with fun practices and exercises aimed at steering the reader toward becoming a tasseo-adept.

Of particular interest to me was her critique of ekphrasis, a term you don't come across every day. In short, ekphrasis refers to the practice of allowing one form of artistic expression, say a great masterpiece, to influence and inspire other creations via active imagination. For example, Tennyson's poem Lady of Shalott and Waterhouse's painting of the same name, or Loreena McKennitt's song.

Such magical synchronicity can be found in tea leaves as well as in poetry and song. The artist (who is you) learns just to let go and become ekphrastic when communing with one's higher self. After all, this is the essence of divination: the discovery and exploration of knowledge that we had no idea we possessed and then, like the Lady of Shalott, we learn to "weave the mirror's magic sights" into our own personal myth.

- Toney Brooks, author of *Chrysalis Tarot Book*

Tabitha Dial's Creative Divination: Read Tea Leaves and Develop Your Personal Code *is a slim book designed to get you working. She doesn't spend a lot of time on the "what tasseomancy" is portion because the meat of the matter is in the practices.*

You can expect to find this book more doing than reading. You could just read it but you would be doing yourself a disservice. Don't buy this book if you are just going to leave it on the shelf. It deserves to be opened and used.

I think you could even use this book as a bit of divination itself. When you don't know which practice to try, just open the book to see where you may be guided.

Dial has given you a chance to be in a workshop with her where you take away all the best parts of her knowledge.

- Arwen Lynch, author of *Mapping the Hero's Journey with Tarot*

DEDICATION

This book is for my family and for everyone who has made space for wonder.

This book is especially for Mom and Dad and my brother Travis, who showed me how to march – and dance – to my own beat. Thank you for helping me find my footing when I need it and for keeping me on my toes.

In memory of loved ones who are gone. In memory, particularly, of my grandmothers, who were good friends. You encouraged and loved our families well. Thank you for your care and guidance.

CONTENTS

ACKNOWLEDGMENTS

Thanks to Ana Maria Selvaggio, a kindred spirit who doesn't fear her muchness. Bubbles of praise and thanks for your bottomless spirit and extensive knowledge. Thank you for taking my manuscript and turning it into an experience more rich and dear than I could've dreamed.

And other Kentucky folk who have helped me feel so at home, including Jerielle Hanlon, Misty Nolan, Beckie and Patrick Henry, Devin Popp, Gretchen Black-Raber, Christina Joy, Eric Murphy, Fran Gautier, Angela Robinson, and Amy Camuglia. Thank you for your kindness, creativity, and contributions to the bluegrass state.

Paige Hankla, the creator of the PlayThink flowmotion festival. Sarabeth Brownrobie, who established Lexpecto Patronum, the local Harry Potter Alliance. And Ellie and Tim Harman, owners and operators of High on Art & Coffee. Without your efforts, many creative people like myself would lack memorable opportunities, or particular groups of like-minded people.

Terri Burch and Rev. Barry White Crow, for inspiring others with their meditations.

i

My current boss in my specialty cheese job, Jason Gillum, for his generosity, innovation, patience, and humor. Thanks for demonstrating tenacity, practicality, and compassion.

Thanks to former bosses Natasha Manning, Brandon Oakley, Eron Barber, Sara Lester, Susan Cohen, Audrey Patterson, and Ashley Mayfield. Your zest for life keep every day lively.

Tarot and divination professionals such as Desi Stern and Kay Braeburn, V Von Schweetz, Hazellie Wong, Benebell Wen, Theresa Reed, Hilary Parry, Toney Brooks, Renna Shesso, Nancy Antenucci, Carrie Paris, Arwen Lynch, Elle North, Paige Zaferiou, Andrew Kyle McGregor, James Wells, Erik C. Dunne, Ashley Story, and Steve Seinberg. Thank you for your dedication, and for welcoming me here and there on your metaphysical and social media journeys.

Special gratitude to Joy Vernon, Sherry Shone, Sherry Hungsberg, Erica Adams, and Jason Lenzini for their mentorship and work with the Denver Tarot Meetup. Your legacies include giving others the chance to teach and learn about tarot, and lenormand, and more, and introducing people to remarkable tarot authors and deck creators.

Familiar faces who share similar interests brighten the world – former and current Denver Tarot Meetup members (especially Linda Bean, Cindy Corbett, Sam Harper, and Danielle Pollack), thanks for all your positivity and love.

Thank you to Mary K Greer for her time talking to me about book publishing at a meal table at TarotCon Denver 2015.

Thank you to Shaheen Miro. Thanks for joyfully encouraging me and for helping shape tea readers, past, present, and future.

Thank you to Goddess Isis Books and Gifts, especially the owner, Karen Charboneau-Harrison. Thank you for hosting and promoting my tea reading party. Thank you for maintaining space for creative divination and exploring spiritual pathways as well as personal codes.

Editors I've worked with as a journalist, a freelancer, and a poet, especially Stephanie G'Schwind, Ian Neligh, Travis Combs, Travis Henry, Fairlight Baer-Gutierrez, Jessy Randall, Marjorie Jensen, Anne Bean, Emily Auger, Nico Mara-McKay, and Deidre Riley. Thanks for encouraging and improving symphonies of voices, including my own.

The teachers and instructors who are too many to mention, particularly Mark Newton, Renee Ruderman, and Dan Beachy-Quick. Thanks for advising me and taking me under your wing. Louann Reed, thanks for introducing graphic novels and video games as multiliteracies: teaching, learning, and communication tools.

Thank you to Sandra Davis McEntire – "It's your life, Tabitha!" – for listening and offering strength as I was ready.

Susan Rowland, Jennifer Selig, and my cohort when I briefly studied depth psychology at Pacifica Graduate institute: Thank you for meeting me where I was, a place where I dreamed my first night on campus that my framed schoolgirl pictures always had a third eye on them – and no one ever thought any different.

Inspiring friends who understand my silliness, and

who let me sing and dance, including Brianna Andrews, Amanda Lee Meredith, Susan Stumbaugh, Kellie Barr, and Amber Clark. Your cups runneth over with great heart and soul, and I'm so lucky to have your wisdom.

Thank you to Alyssa Rice and Kayla Kidwell-Snyder for being my first tea leaf reading assistants.

Special thanks to Chris Brunson for your support.

Thank you to those with whom I have shared my home, hopes, and dreams. Our time together brought me new perspective and enriched my personal code.

And you, the readers of this book. As Metro State University of Denver professor Sandra Doe says, "it is an honor for your work to be seen. Thanks for the read."

Life is meant, in part, for good questions and places to ask them.

CREATIVE DIVINATION

Coworker: She tells people's futures.

Me: I wouldn't go that far.
People's futures are their own.

Introduction to Creative Divination

Developing divination skills and creativity is like hosting a pretend tea party. They involve flexibility and openness. For me, the idea of creative divination is about welcoming trusted friends to the table, but saving a seat for surprise guests. As you create or divine, your best tools are your imagination and ability to cast aside all your preconceived notions.

What is divination? It is related to fortune telling, but arguably more of an exercise in reflection and self-improvement. A diviner uses their tools (like cards, crystals, runes, tea leaves, and more) to understand their surroundings and perceive one version of a clear present and a desired future.

A willingness to sit still and yet giggle freely with first responses is the sort of approach that resonates in this book. Maybe you had intentions of reading tea but your imagination was sparked by the experience and now that pirate ship that you saw in the bottom of your cup has you doing an art project or writing a poem. This is a perfect example of creative divination! Run wild!

Psychics (or diviners) and creative people, both known to see and interpret situations with vision that may puzzle others, may or may not always know the rules of their discipline, or heed them. This book encourages everyone to break rules – to explore, to ponder, to create. This is not a dictionary of tea leaf symbols or a step-by-step instruction manual for the art of tea leaf reading (tasseomancy).

By reading tea leaves, anyone can soak in a wide range of information. For example, anyone can:

- Encounter our frustrations
- Glimpse our mindscape
- Break through on the matters that weigh on us
- Better understand our needs and emotions
- Uncover new avenues that take us to our hopes and fears

Preparing to read tea, then, is a meditative and/or psychological undertaking. Intentionally birthing something, wanting to reconcile a relationship, seeking solace: All can be approached through a tea reading, or by using the structure in this book as inspiration.

How to Use this Book

Use this book as you feel called to. Do everything in each practice or just whatever you're drawn to at the time. Feel intimidated? Practices twenty-eight, twenty-nine, and sixty-four are great places to start training your mind.

Feel free to go through all the creative divination, and do whichever one calls to you, or do them in succession.

A phrase may catch your eye and that's all the inspiration you need. Don't hold back and never define yourself with anyone else's language.

Tea leaf reading means finding your personal code.

Creative divination is your gift. And your creative divination is about your whim as much as it is about your ritual.

Interview fairies. Bury hatchets. Sit with ancestors and warriors.

What I've hoped to write is a collection of tea leaf reading methods, with inspiration on how to use the tools of the cup and the tea images themselves. Each exercise is intended to be adapted for any creative or intuitive, psychological, or holistic discipline.

It is my dream that these exercises will spark conversations with the soul – and more so, foster healing and new art, new writing, new songs, new hope. You may sit for a time with any or every practice reading and sketch or chant or sing or take notes.

May you always feel welcome to play and never fear looking into your world for something more.

Basics of Tea Leaf Readings

There are many ways to **prepare a cup of tea for interpretation**. None of them are wrong, but it is recommended loose leaf tea is used, preferably tea that isn't heavy with flavor enhancing items like lemongrass or bits of fruit. I find flower petals an exception. Basic rule: Use a tea you love and one that is made of material that is fluid (easily floats and curls and unfurls).

I prefer to put the loose tea directly into the cup. This is important because it allows the tea to cling to the cup when ready for interpretation.

The roundness of tea cups allows for interpretations from all angles. Don't have a fortune teller's cup? While seemingly helpful, it's preferable that your cup is free of markings that designate what tea remnants can be read where and how.

When at a tea leaf reading party, I encourage guests to enjoy their tea together. Originally, tea was not brewed and strained when it was consumed. If anyone does not like to drink with tea floating in their cup, I happily use a small strainer.

For the sake of time and so I do not feel I start coloring the reading through small talk or such, my reference is to perform a brief grounding exercise with my client using their tea leaves in their cup as a focal point. Then I strain the cup and begin to interpret it. You may choose to sip your tea and contemplate the needs and desires of the reading.

Your Personal Code: Suggestions on Tea Leaf Reading Symbols

Tea leaf readings are a lot like cloud gazing. We see what we see based on our life experiences. We see what we see because of our expectations, both positive and negative.

Common imagery includes **animals, letters, numbers**, and **geometric shapes**.

If you've spent your youth drawn towards something, it may often resurface in tea leaves: for instance, I've found **dancers, mystical creatures**, and **trees** and **birds** and **bridges/rainbows** in many tea cups.

Modern references are valid and powerful. Images don't have to feel epic, special, or ancient to have meaning. Mario and Kirby, **video game characters**, have appeared in readings, and so has a **superhero** with a cape. **Cartoon characters** and figures from **movies** and **tv** are engaging and enlightening, too. For a creative divination practice that looks in detail at cartoon characters, see practice 63.

Often, when your subconscious knows it is facing a pattern it must break, other images will be more pronounced. Some of these may incorporate parts of your life that were important when you were in your early youth, or at another milestone in life. For example, **religious symbols, hearts** and **particular flowers, specific animals, cars, tools of a new trade, music notes** and **instruments, sport-related imagery, astrological symbols** of people who impacted you, and so on.

6

Treat images personally. The flag symbol has emerged for me as a reminder of how my teen years were spent. **Flags on flagpoles** represent my dedication to Color Guard and marching band in high school. The common interpretations of a flag in tea include loyalty to a cause or country, and red flag warnings.

Gaining an eye for tea leaf reading grants you a visual map, too, to confirm that you are on the right path. Just as I dream of marching band during points in my life when my sense of belonging, and creativity and passion are transitioning, I might see a rose next to a flag: "Stop and smell the roses to enhance your sense of belonging and identity."

The nature of all symbols/signals depends on what other symbols appear in the cup. Could that lion be the Leo in your life? Or does it indicate time, as in the month of August? It may be clear instantly. The answer may surface over time.

Intuition, Faith, and Inspiration

The enemy of divination is forced thinking or overanalyzing. Intuition is often deceptively illogical.

It can come across as gobbledygook when it's allowed to flow easily.

And to get the most out of a tea leaf session, there's no time for second-guessing.

Rely on your instinct. Go with your first thoughts.

This includes opening your mouth and describing things that may not readily seem to appear to others. Your definitions need not fit anyone else's.

For many, the shapes in tea leaves don't make much sense, especially as a beginning reader.

But if you are receiving messages you feel prompted to share as you look at the cup, do so. Another way of putting this technique is called channeling or scrying.

I've uttered the words, "I'm getting the idea/feeling of a [fill in the blank] in this area of the cup.". It could be an animal you had as a pet. It could be a more complex concept, like an impression of someone engaged in an activity. Or you might feel an emotion or a sensation during the reading – while centered for the reading, quickly determine if that feeling is meant for you or the person you are reading. Then use that insight as appropriate.

It all relates.

Readings that are spontaneous and heartfelt have profound impact. They don't need to be weighed down with detailed evidence and solid argument.

Consider yourself a poet. A dreamy cloud gazer. The beauty of tea reading is that it is so highly interpretive.

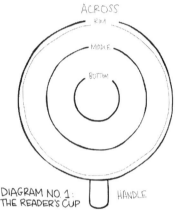

DIAGRAM NO. 1:
THE READER'S CUP

You may focus your breathing and imagine your energy going to the core of the Earth.

Begin each reading with faith. Start talking.

Relax and set preconceptions and self-judgment aside.

Location, Location, Location

Translating a tea cup also requires awareness of the size and location of symbols: If most the image is prominent, or images tend toward one area of the cup, that can indicate an obsession or obstacle.

The handle stands for what you are holding onto or what you take responsibility for. The space directly across from it can be interpreted as innate abilities or gifts coming your way. In the creative divination practice exercises, these positions are referred to as **Handle** and **Across**.

Many readers see the **bottom of the cup** as the future, but as a developing tasseomancer, I met Shaheen Miro through the Denver Tarot Meetup and appreciate his interpretation that the bottom of the cup is the past and adapted that technique. We cannot much avoid our pasts, after all, and the bottom of the cup can be a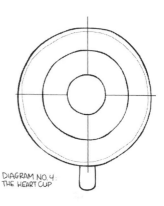

DIAGRAM NO. 4
THE HEART CUP

unavoidable surface. I often see the bottom of the cup, too, as a theme that needs investigated or respected during a reading.

The **middle of the cup** connotes the present situation.

As you climb toward the **rim of the cup**, the images speak more to the future. If there are leaves on the outside of the cup, this could be something truly metaphysical. Many leaves on the rim can mean the seeker of the reading puts a lot of stock in future possibilities.

Further, where the symbols, and the size of them, unfold in relation to the left (feminine, receptive), the right (masculine, active), and the handle of the cup, at the bottom, middle, or rim of the cup, can refine meaning. A diamond in the middle, left side of the cup could be interpreted as:

1. concern about long-term financial stability and the finer things in life – a desire to have something lasting (the diamond)
2. in one's present day (the middle of the cup, as opposed to the bottom or the rim)

3. while living a compassionate lifestyle (the left side of the cup).

You may use the standard Reader positions, which include the middle, handle, and rim, as suggested throughout most of the practice examples, but feel free to experiment with The Heart Configuration (above) in Practice 51.

The point is that you find a style that works for you.

PART ONE: Reading FOR

The most accessible approach to creative divination is to present each practice/reading for an audience- or towards an end goal or desire.

Imagine a person, or enjoy your volunteers or clients. You can always practice on yourself.

In this section are practice readings for different goals and other purposes. Themes include connecting to animal allies, sharing your hero's journey, providing healing or comfort, and more. One of the common reasons folks see a psychic is for insight on their love lives. That approach is covered in this section.

Read for self-improvement.
Read for entertainment.
Read for a friend.

Remember: Tea leaf reading is a gift, as all art should be, to paraphrase Mark Eleveld's thoughts on slam poetry, in the book and CD *The Spoken Word Revolution*.

Practice 1:
WITH A LITTLE HELP FROM YOUR FRIENDS

Even if your goal while using this book is to be able to wow friends, family, and strangers with your tea leaf reading skills, looking for your friends and allies in your tea cup for yourself is one of the most rewarding practices offered by this art form.

It is one of the most fun gifts tea leaf reading offers.

You may begin this practice reading by *trying this* **meditation**:

Get comfortable. Imagine you are preparing for a road trip that will last into the night or longer.

List in your mind all the items you want with you. What food and drinks do you need? What will provide you comfort and support? How will you stay alert and entertained?

Finally, who do you want with you and what type of transportation are you using?

Imagine packing it all up.

Begin the reading.

Formatted around part of the Hero's Journey, here are the positions in the cup and how you may wish to interpret what appears in each:

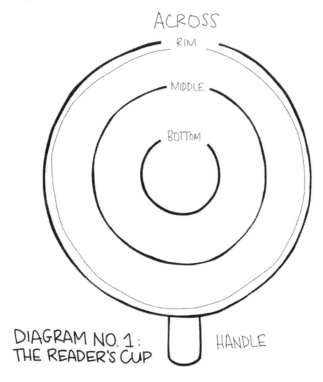

DIAGRAM NO. 1:
THE READER'S CUP

Bottom: Tests and Allies -- what are you being asked to work on or overcome in your life right now, and who is helping you?

Handle: Approach -- how you and your newfound allies prepare for this challenge

Across: The Ordeal -- what death or fear can your allies help you with?

Middle: The Reward -- what treasure or treasures have your allies helped you find?

Rim: The Road Back -- how can you bring your allies (or their lessons) home with you?

After your practice reading: Review your answers to the questions in the optional exercise about finding "yes". Do your descriptive words apply to the allies and friends that appeared in your practice reading? How so?

Unfold this reading: Let reality guide you. What friends have you made in different eras and areas of your life?

Read with the goal of paying attention to the lesson one particular friend shared. You may start by listing five different friends:

- One from childhood
- One from your years as a teenager
- One who was a fellow performer, musician, athlete, artist, family member, etc
- One who knew you as a young adult
- One who has moved away (or who you have moved away from)

See how the spirit of your friendship influences your interpretation of this tea leaf reading practice.

INSIGHTS
Question or Focus (if any)

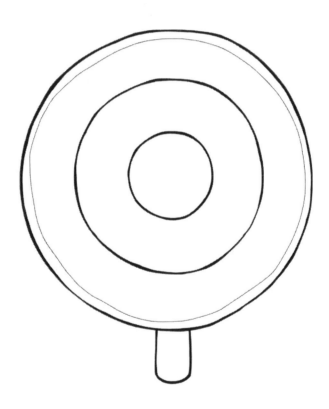

Practice 2:
MAKE TEA, NOT WAR

Not all of us are buddies! Sometimes the company we keep isn't the easiest to have around. This practice tea leaf reading helps in finding common ground – whether you are butting heads at home, still struggle with a parent as an adult, or have troubles with coworkers, look to your tea leaves for things you may have in common.

Bottom: The relationship as it is right now
Handle: How you see the issues you are encountering
Across: How the other person(s) views the same issues
Middle: What you can do to find your own peace with this pattern
Rim: What you need to leave behind

Unfold this reading: Can you take a symbol, such as an animal or letter or number, a musical instrument or shape of a state or a country, and create an object?

Perhaps carve key images onto a candle, and burn it as you set your intention to find peace in the situation you had in mind during the reading.

Or an animal appeared in the reading: Create a small one from clay or buy a figurine at a thrift store, and bury it. Bury that hare like a hatchet.

INSIGHTS
Question or Focus (if any)

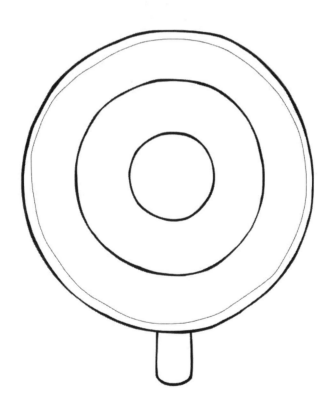

Practice 3:
INTERVIEW WITH A FAIRY

Animals, dancers, mythic figures and non-sentient objects appear often in tea leaves. But why are they there, and what do they want?

This brief interview can get you on your way to understanding them and their role in your present day life. Adapt this exercise to engage any animal, performer, mythic figure, or symbol/object that you want to know more about.

Bottom: How does this fairy like to present itself?
Handle: What would it like you to do for it?
Across: What does it need you to know about itself that may surprise you?
Middle: What is their purpose in their world?
Rim: What do they offer to you now?

How do you like your tea?

You may also want to ask these questions and any others you invent:

If this fairy has an outfit, what does it look like?
What kind of wings does it have, and what color?
Does it work with any of my spirit allies?
What does it think about my spirit allies?
When did it start appearing in my life?

Unfold this reading: This reading helps you identify signs of fairy life, and can easily adapt to any interest. Give it a try with a mind towards understanding:

Dragons
Magical ponies
Shamanic figures
Spirit allies
Time travelers
Aliens or adventurers in space
Animal messengers

INSIGHTS
Question or Focus (if any)

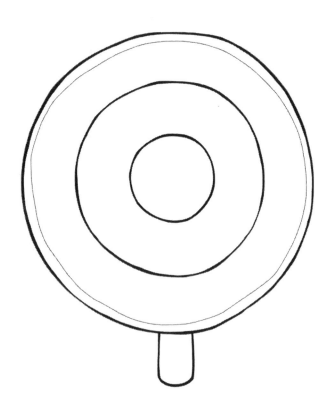

Practice 4:
COMMUNICATE WITH YOUR SPIRIT ALLIES

You may have one or two main spirit allies, and plenty of others. Some appear at different times for different purposes.

If you aren't familiar with your spirit ally, *try the following* **meditation**, adapted from Rev. Barry White Crow:

Close your eyes in a comfortable, safe place where you won't be disturbed.

Take a few long, deep breaths.

Imagine you are in a forest. It is lush and cool. The sun shines on a mossy pathway. You can feel it beneath your feet and you walk forward.

The trees grow larger.

You are safe and at peace with yourself. You do not have to pretend to be anyone or anything, no one is here to ask anything of you.

The path leads to a large tree with a large hole in it. As you get closer, you see the hole is large enough for you to enter.

You enter the tree and begin to walk down, and down, and down, into the cool earth. It is quiet and heals you with unconditional love.

You see another small path and follow it to the opening of a cave. You step inside. Here you can see and hear your spirit guide.

You carefully look at this guide so you can remember what it looks like. You may ask it what its message is for you now. You may tell it your name and listen for its response.

Stay here for as long as you need.

Imagine offering a gift to your spirit guide. It can be anything. It can be a lock of hair or a lost treasure from your past.

When you are ready and have thanked this guide for being with you, return to the entrance of the cave.

Walk down the path.

Go up inside the earth.

Stand inside the tree.

Leave the tree and return to the long, mossy path.

Carefully leave the woods.

Here is how you may interpret your tea cup to further your encounters with your spirit allies:

Bottom: What is the nature of the one spirit ally who wishes to communicate today?
Handle: How can I be considerate of this spirit ally?
Across: What is this spirit ally showing me today?
Middle: How will I improve my life by working with this spirit ally?
Rim: Possible future gifts

INSIGHTS
Question or Focus (if any)

_____

_____

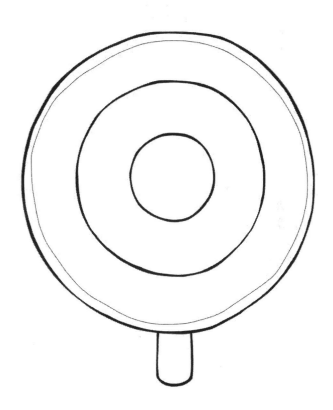

Practice 5:
READ FOR A NEW FRIEND

You have just found yourself in the company of an immediate, kindred spirit. They vibe with your vibe. They march at a similar pace, or have a similar flair. You mesh.

You gotta hang out!

Here's a reading to get to know them and show them love.

Bottom: What you both bring to your new relationship
Handle: What your new friend's best friendship trait is right now
Across: How you respond to this particular friendship trait
Middle: What you have in common
Rim: Where your friendship may be heading, and suggested activities or conversations to share

Tip: *Don't forget to look at negative space (the open space between the leaves).*

INSIGHTS
Question or Focus (if any)

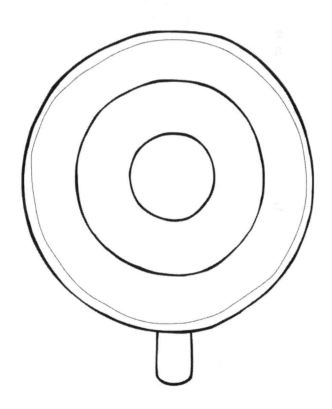

Practice 6:
READ FOR AN OLD FRIEND OR FAMILY LEGACY

Old, tried and true friends can be wonderful! Family legacy can act as gravity and glue.

Option One: If you have positive and deep unwavering feelings about your old friends and/or family legacy, try this practice reading:

Bottom: What you and your old friend have in common
Handle: The good things that you give to your relationship
Across: How to remain a valuable friend (this may mean you need to ask for more or offer to do less)
Middle: The patterns that need to be repeated until you learn from them (in other words, the challenges and benefits that may come of having this relationship, or one with someone who reminds you of this person)
Rim: How you can remain loving to yourselves

Option Two: Sometimes, we need to filter out our nostalgia to better our lives and not repeat past mistakes or fail at being our best selves due to the legacies of others.

To help heal and move away from this relationship:

Bottom: What you and your old friend still have in common
Handle: The good things that came from your relationship
Across: How to let go of anything that needs to be let go of
Middle: The patterns that need to repeat until you learn from them (in other words, the challenges and benefits that may come of having this relationship, or one with someone who reminds you of this person)
Rim: How you can remain loving to yourself

Option Three: You may be uncertain of your relationship with an old friend, or how you are coping with a family legacy. To help understand this relationship:

Bottom: How you and the old friend or family legacy are undeniably alike
Handle: How you are responsible for your perceptions about this relationship
Across: How to let go of anything that needs to be let go of
Middle: What you need to still understand about this relationship
Rim: How you can remain loving to yourself

INSIGHTS
Question or Focus (if any)

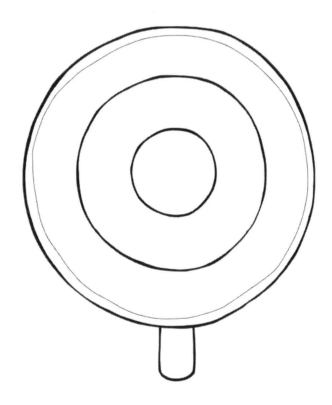

Practice 7:
READ FOR A FAVORITE FAMILY
OR COMMUNITY MEMBER

Our favorite family and community members often are people we tend to identify with, or wish to aspire to be like.

You have built some relationship with them. And you get to build some of the structure you may use for this practice tea leaf reading, too.

First, list three traits that you feel they inspire you to bring out in yourself.

Now, what one situation could they talk about that would make you think less of them?

Finally, what do you think keeps the pair of you connected (outside of the community or family that brought you together)?

Bottom: How does this tell you something new about how you are connected?

Handle: What can you do today because they inspire you?

Across: How can they continue to inspire you tomorrow?

Middle: What can you confront together (this relates to what they might talk about that might make you think less of them)?

Rim: How can you remain connected

When he wrote us letters and things, Uncle Scott liked to add a little T-rex head after his signature. Dinosaurs turn up often in my tea leaf readings. Even if they aren't the king of the dinosaurs, they certainly echo my uncle's character and an interest in discovery.

INSIGHTS
Question or Focus (if any)

_____

_____

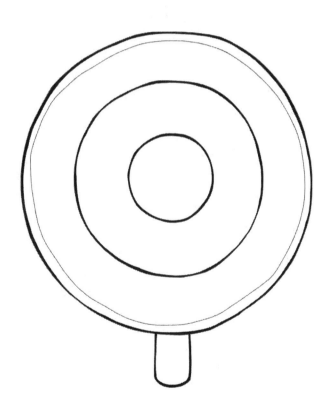

Practice 8:
READ THE MIDDLE WAY

Read in honor of someone who illustrates balance, not influenced by one tenant or another. Someone who reminds you of inner peace. If no one comes to mind, consider someone who seems comfortable in their body and who seems quick to laugh innocently and joyfully.

The Buddhist concept of the *Middle Way* is that moderation is a path of wisdom: Neither self-indulgence nor self-denial nor self-discipline as devotion to religion.

Bottom: Where in your life do you need to work on finding the Middle Way?

Handle: How can someone who inspires you to be balanced give you a beginning on this path of wisdom?

Across: Like a dancer or tight-rope walker, where do you need to keep looking so you don't fall off-balance?

Middle: How are you existing in the middle of your mind, body, heart, and soul?

Rim: What can you leave behind, today, to reminding yourself of your spirit, your awakening?

INSIGHTS
Question or Focus (if any)

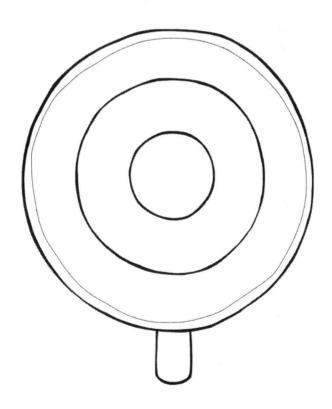

Practice 9:
READ FOR A HERMIT

If you were to enter a hermit's world and you wanted to inspire them, how would you try to read their tea leaves?

Bottom: How the hermit lights up their world
Handle: What the hermit does to sustain their current status
Across: How they feel about the outside world
Middle: What they can do with and for the outside world
Rim: Highlights of the next stage in their life

You'll find that your perceptions of someone who lives alone will influence the images you see, or how you determine their meaning.

Do you feel you respect or pity the typical hermit?

Unfold this reading: Try this as a reading where you look for messages FROM a hermit, giving examples of wisdom and insight.

INSIGHTS
Question or Focus (if any)

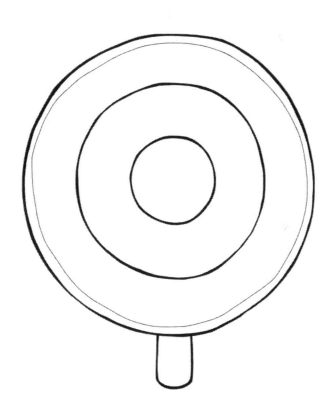

Practice 10:
READ FOR LOVE

Whether self-love or love with a romantic partner, it can be a big challenge to obtain, maintain, and/or sustain love.

Bottom: What you can do to help yourself gain, give, or receive love
Handle: Where to begin stretching yourself
Across: What you require from others
Middle: What compromises you must make
Rim: What to leave behind

Unfold this reading: Apply this reading to other principles, such as kindness, patience, and being humble.

INSIGHTS
Question or Focus (if any)

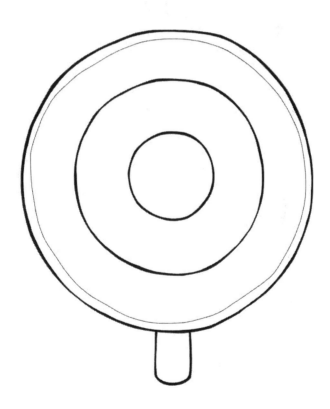

Practice 11:
READ FOR YOUR INNER CHILD

Our inner child is one of our purest muses. They create without reservation, because they don't have an inner-judge criticizing them. They seek to learn and play. And they give their gifts with great love.

Here is a **meditation** *and* practice reading to help you reach out to your inner child and get an idea for how to celebrate him/her/zir.

Meditation *for your inner child*:

You have not been born, but you have selected the life lessons you want. You have created a blueprint for this life. You have been careful.
Take a deep breath in, respecting the life you have become and are becoming.
Hold it for a moment.
Release it, with gratitude for the weight of the lessons you have had.
Take a deep breath in, acknowledging that you are the protector of your inner child.
Hold it for a moment.

Release it, releasing any guilt you may have about your responsibilities to your inner child.

Take a deep breath in, asking your inner child to make itself more present in your life.
Hold it for a moment.
Release it, and relax into the vision of holding your inner child's hand in yours.
Now, observe your parents, before you were born. Watch them climb different parts of a mountain until they meet. It is here that you are created.
Your inner child gets your attention. Does he/she/ze tug at your clothing? Giggle? Sing? Whisper?
You have a glimpse of your inner child's core.
You exchange gifts.
You find yourself in a home on the mountain. It is safe and peaceful. You rest here until you are ready to leave.
You leave and return to your daily life.

Option One: Time to play

Bottom: What does your inner child experience?
Handle: What does your inner child want you to create or learn?
Across: What does your inner child want you to give away?
Middle: How can you play with your inner child?
Rim: How can you bring your inner child into the world on an everyday basis?

Option Two: A small gift

Bottom: What gift has your inner child given you?
Handle: How can you value this gift?
Across: How can you share this gift with others?
Middle: Who/where will your inner child and these gifts be best valued?
Rim: How can you thank your inner child?

INSIGHTS
Question or Focus (if any)

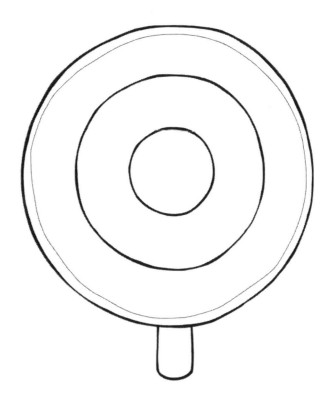

Practice 12:
READ FOR A RISK-TAKER

Who inspired you to take risks? Imagine them and read for them. What symbols of courage, if any, do you see in the tea leaves?

Bottom: Is there a risk you are resisting?
Handle: How does your most-admired risk taker handle risks?
Across: What do you need to look out for (if there's anything in this spot, now is probably not the best time to take this risk, at least not without input from professionals)?
Middle: Where might this risk lead you?
Rim: How can you balance adventure and practicality?

INSIGHTS
Question or Focus (if any)

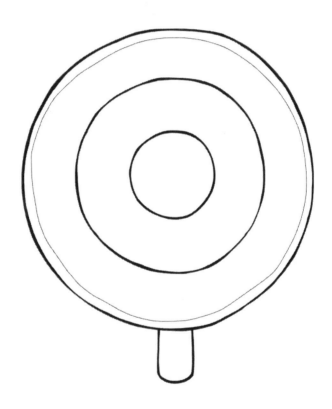

Practice 13:
READ FOR THE STARS

You can read for that which lies beyond or the great mysteries of life. Or you can interpret this style of reading as an opportunity to read for a local or world-renowned celebrity. Who is your favorite entertainer?

Bottom: What is the issue at hand for the person receiving this reading?
Handle: What do they need to do now for best results?
Across: What is their next step?
Middle: How do they spread their light into the universe?
Rim: What is the possible outcome of the issue at hand?

Unfold this reading: Try this reading for both the first entertainer you remember being enamored with and the type of entertainer you think you'll always enjoy.

My first entertainer, for example, comes from early childhood. Like lots of children in the United States, I liked Sesame Street and I have a strong memory of seeing Grover on the television in the hospital where I had an appendectomy at the age of five. He always seemed to appear before my doctor, who I recollect having the name Dr. Grover, arrived to check on me.

INSIGHTS
Question or Focus (if any)

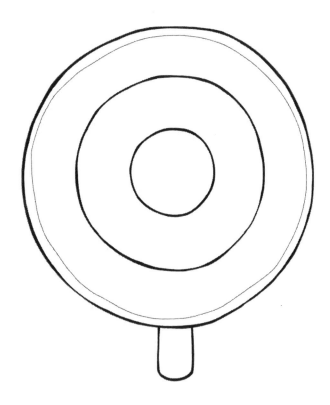

Practice 14:
HONOR AN OLD FAMILY FRIEND

In the dark months following the deaths of my grandmothers, who died within three months of each other, I had a dream. In it, I heard a voice (when this clairaudience comes, I listen, especially after what happened in this story!): "Get in touch with June".

I was sure it was a friend of my grandmother's! And I asked my aunt and uncle and my mother, but no one connected the name to an individual. It wasn't quite June yet, but that had to work as an answer – be in touch with nature.

After a few weeks, my aunt remembered: June *was* a very good friend, and yes, here was her phone number. I gave her a call. She was grateful to hear from one of the grandchildren she had met and heard so much about. She'd been at the funeral.

We talked a handful of times since the first call, and she was, in those moments, a surrogate grandmother, and a connection to my hometown.

Think of someone who has been on the periphery of your life, if you don't have a family friend who was present in your childhood life or among any of your children as they've grown. An old family friend could be a pet, too, or a neighbor.

Bottom: What, from your past, is important right now?
Handle: What can you keep from this lesson that is of benefit to yourself?
Across: What part of your past is helpful, now, to others?
Middle: Information about the present day
Rim: Possible future outcomes

INSIGHTS
Question or Focus (if any)

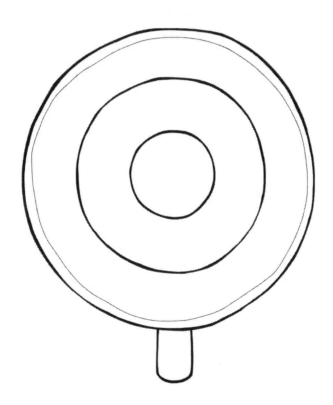

Practice 15:
READ THE SEASON AHEAD

With this practice reading, you will look into the next few months for whoever you need to practice reading for. Remember that when you learn, you are often your most immediate person to practice on!

This can be a broad reading, such as what the summer tour for a particular musician will be like. Or it may be more precise. What will happen this fall at work (which is still a very broad question, granted, but not so broad as the summer tour)? What can I expect romantically this spring? How's this winter going to be?

Bottom: What this season has in store, on a broad level
Handle: What I can do to be prepared
Across: Details from the season ahead
Middle: Any information that might make this season memorable
Rim: How the season before this one will influence it

INSIGHTS
Question or Focus (if any)

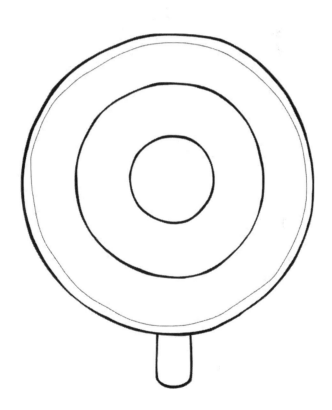

Practice 16:
READ THE WHEEL OF THE YEAR

For this reading, you'll **divide the cup into eight equal parts**, starting from the handle. You may divide the cup a number of ways. Your first position (the handle of the tea cup) may be:

1) Midsummer
2) The celebration closest to your birthday
3) The celebration closest to the current time of year

To divide the cup, imagine cutting the circle into four even pieces. Then imagine that the spaces in between those are also moments in time to interpret.

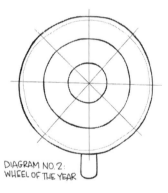

DIAGRAM NO. 2:
WHEEL OF THE YEAR

Unfold this reading: Simplify this reading by reading only for the "quarter days" – the Solstices and Equinoxes (the four seasons).

INSIGHTS
Question or Focus (if any)

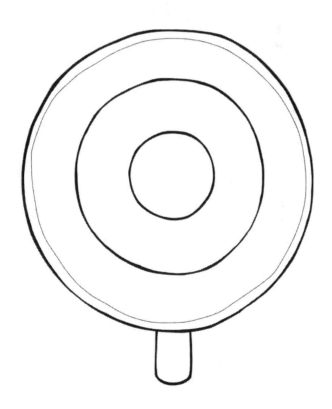

Practice 17:
LOOK FOR EVIDENCE OF A PAST LIFE

Why not use tea leaves to find clues of past lives?
Look, in particular, for:

1) any **animals**
2) any hints of **landscapes** or **architecture**, like
   distinctive **homes**, **bridges**, **hills**, **mountains**,
   rivers, **oceans**
3) **letters** or **numbers**

All of these might help with a time and place that
you once lived.

Bottom: Foundation – landscape, language or
heritage
Handle: Home Role – were you a caregiver, a youth,
a hunter-gatherer, a storyteller?
Across: Community Position – were you a leader, a
teacher, a messenger, a baker, a tailor, a candlestick
maker?
Middle: Life Lessons – What themes from this life
show your greatest struggles and strengths?
Rim: Acing Today's Tests – What themes from then
can you benefit from now?

INSIGHTS
Question or Focus (if any)

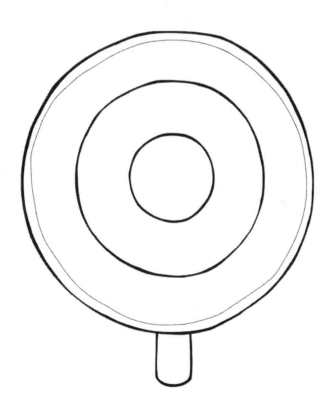

Practice 18:
UNDERSTAND SORROW

A common human experience is sorrow. We lose people, places, our sense of self.

If we aren't careful, sorrow can become a trap. Resist becoming stuck by addressing your emotions and the possible source of them. There is always a lot to uncover about the complexity of every situation.

Bottom: What you may need to know about you or your seeker's sorrow

Handle: What you can let go of

Across: How you can make your sorrow into something positive. Where do you need to be the most patient right now?

Middle: The possibilities and lessons your sorrow gives you now. What is this teaching you about suffering or obstacles?

Rim: Ways of overcoming the sorrow that may not have been already suggested

Tip: *Water droplets commonly remain in tea cups during interpretation. Accept them as signs of genuine release - often emotional. Consider where they lie in the cup to determine when they have or will occur. Look for shapes in nearby tea leaves for more insight.*

INSIGHTS
Question or Focus (if any)

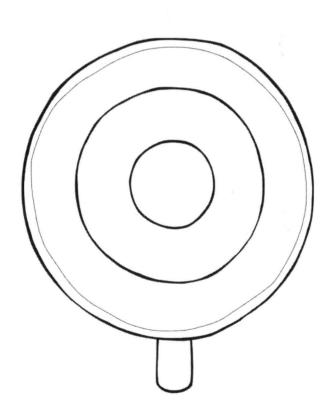

Practice 19:
DETERMINE HOW TO IMPROVE YOUR KARMA

Divide the cup into two parts: One half with the handle in the middle of it.

- The half with the handle in it represents the karma that you have changed in your life.
- The half on the opposite side represents the karma that you need to work on.

DIAGRAM NO. 3:
THE SPLIT CUP

How can you use the skills and information represented in the first half? How do those symbols work with the second half?

INSIGHTS
Question or Focus (if any)

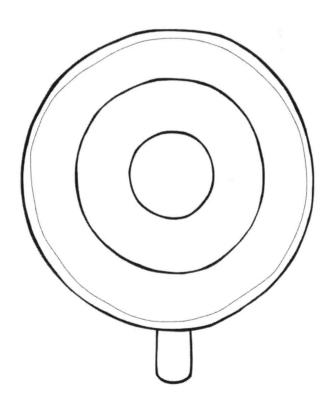

Practice 20:
CONNECT TO YOUR STORY

Dive into this cup looking for signs of where you are in your own story now. You may focus on things like a beginning, middle, an end, and a plot twist (if you really like plot twists, the next practice reading might be an ideal substitute). Maybe you are interested in characters in your life right now. Or you feel disconnected to your life's purpose or story.

Write down the goal of connecting to your story with this practice reading, along with 1-3 steps or things to look for to get you to your goal.

Then begin.

Like always, you may decide to use this outline, but you don't need to:

Bottom: The origins of your story
Handle: How you see your story right now
Across: How others see your story right now
Middle: The present part of your story
Rim: Where your story is going next

INSIGHTS
Question or Focus (if any)

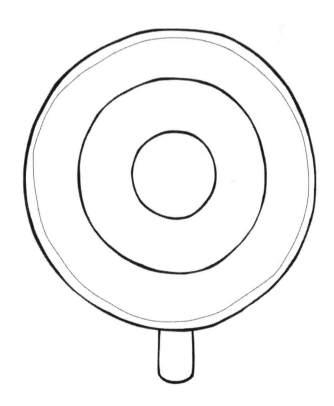

Practice 21:
REVEAL YOUR HIDDEN NATURE

On the inside, you're different than you may seem on the exterior. In other words: What's at the core of the Earth, what might erupt, given certain conditions?

Your hidden nature, here, is not quite your shadow side, which gets its own explanation and practice reading. This is your own personal plot twist.

Bottom: What do you need to know about your hidden nature, now?
Handle: What do you crave?
Across: What do you want to let go of right now?
Middle: How do you and your hidden nature work together?
Rim: What lesson can you take away from your hidden nature right now?

Unfold this reading: If you are interested in astrology, this practice reading ties in well with your ascendant or rising sign. You may choose to read or use this creative divination with this in mind. for example if your rising sign is Gemini, you may choose to read for the archetype of someone who craves communication, travel, stimulation, and yet who may be a bit duplicitous.

INSIGHTS
Question or Focus (if any)

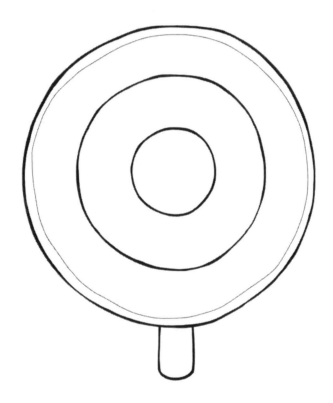

Practice 22:
UNFOLD NEW IDEAS ABOUT YOUR NEEDS

Struggle with making special purchases for yourself or others? Do you carelessly spend time and other resources, or feel uncomfortable with how rarely you utilize them?

Maybe you need someone to look after you. Or maybe it's time to open your heart again. Or apply for another job. Or move to a better (possibly downsized, or safer) location.

Take a moment to meditate on what it is you feel you need right now. Write down a few ideas, and even plan a little to manifest your needs. Give yourself five minutes.

Bottom: What you need now
Handle: Your role in getting what you need
Across: What blocks you
Middle: Anything in your environment that can help you with what you need
Rim: Ideas on how to work toward what you need

Tip: *When animals appear in readings, especially ones with a focus on reviewing personal needs, pay attention to their behavior. How do they find food? Do they hunt alone or in packs? Do they forage? Are they scavengers? What type of patience and planning do they show, and how does this relate to what you need in your life?*

INSIGHTS
Question or Focus (if any)

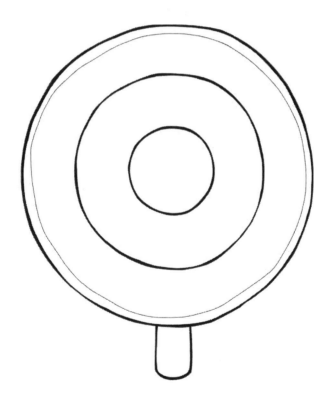

Practice 23:
STIR UP SYMBOLS OF PERSONAL STRENGTH

Whether you or someone you know is going through a personal trial, it helps to have your own symbols of strength to get you past it all!
Look for those symbols here.
Possible images include **eagles, lions, stars, snails** (Why not? Why not any hard-shelled creature?), any **predatory animals, houses, squares, trees, shields**, and **pens** and **swords**.
If symbols appear in your reading that make you question the concept of strength in them, write about that. Or discuss it with a friend or a pet.

Tip: *Let your personal code develop however the tea leaves see fit. Go with first impressions. If the images you see don't seem to conform to an expectation you have, don't force it, but let their power sit for a night, a week, a month. Remember that what might seem like a weakness or smallness is often an indication of strength. The image of a delicate sprout shows courage and growth. An egg or heart that has cracked open fosters new life or the invitation to heal and gain empathy for others, respectively.*

INSIGHTS
Question or Focus (if any)

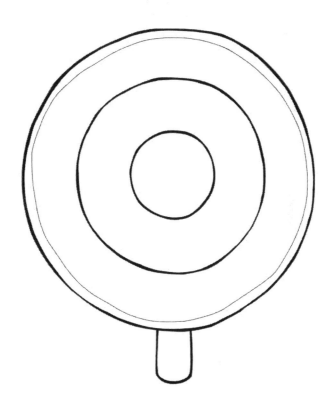

Practice 24:
FIND YOUR ANIMAL ALLY

If you have an animal you have a strong connection to, read with that animal in mind.

If you don't have one animal, or you don't know what animal could be your ally, read to find out which one is working with you now.

Tip: *Animal allies want to help you make the most of your intentions. When you can focus your intention with precision, you'll find that your results are more useful. Be as clear as you can with what you want help with before you begin this reading.*

Bottom: The foundation and core of this animal (its feet or underbelly, and its skeleton, if it has one)
Handle: The trait you have that it is attracted to
Across: The trait you have that it asks you to work on
Middle: How this animal appears to you on a daily basis, and how it is working with you
Rim: How to move in and out of this animal ally's world

INSIGHTS
Question or Focus (if any)

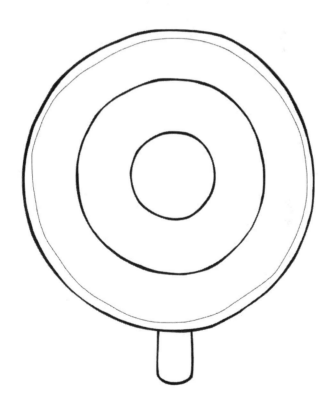

Practice 25:
READ FOR YOUR VALUE

Different than reading for symbols of personal strength, here you get to see what makes you such an asset to your community, and why you are a treasure.

This creative divination exercise isn't so much about inner reflection as it is about how you can help in your community. The symbols you may find can correlate with your role in your family, and your own home, or at work.

Look for symbols that correspond with avatars and screen names. For example, you may see a **dragonfly** or **loin cloth**.

Bottom: What you need to know about your value now

Handle: How you can improve your relationship with your value

Across: Anything surprising and delightful you may not expect

Middle: How your value is evolving and how others see your value

Rim: Any other thoughts

Tip: *People's perceptions are often foggy, misunderstood, even ever-changing. Including your own. Take these impressions about your value – and anyone else's – with a forgiving attitude. Love and improve yourself. Use how you feel about this practice reading as a possible larger message about your boundaries.*

INSIGHTS
Question or Focus (if any)

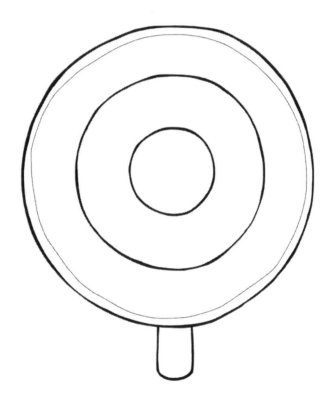

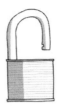

Practice 26:
RECOGNIZE YOUR FEAR

The opposite of fear is freedom. Be mindful that your fear doesn't become a crushing force in your life.

If you're finding it difficult to gain perspective or back away from a fear that is crippling you, it may or may not be a good time to address your fear. However, insight into your fear can prove beneficial.

Tip: *Do your best to focus only on what is right in front of you on the road ahead, not four or five turns down the road.*

Bottom: What your fear really is
Handle: What you can or cannot do about it right now
Across: What your higher power or spirit allies can do about it
Middle: How you can let go of this fear
Rim: Steps you need to remain mindful of to release this fear

Unfold this reading: What symbols appeared in this creative divination that you feel best represents your fear at this time? Write a story or fairy tale using these objects.

For example, a flute could be cursed, or a hat, when worn, might transform yourself or your thoughts.

Make yourself the hero of a story where you overcome fear as a symbol. Include a scene where you either transform the object that represents your fear, are you lovingly hand it over to a mentor or a higher power.

INSIGHTS
Question or Focus (if any)

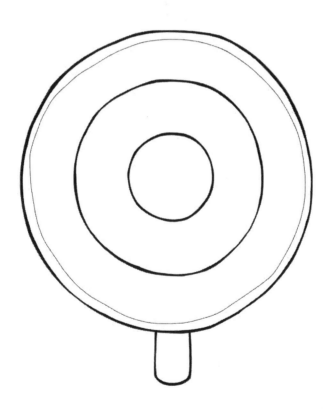

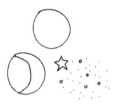

Practice 27:
READ FOR THE SUN, MOON, STARS

This reading can be done once with a mindset for what naturally lights your days and nights. Or it can be done as a 3-parter.

As three parts:

The Sun: Read for what illuminates your day (or week) ahead. It can be a search for the joy and innocence you'll experience. You may want to designate one area as a "red flag zone" – things to watch out for and avoid.

The Moon: Read for what keeps you full, mysterious, dreamy. If you are reading when the moon is full or when it is getting full, what can you manifest? If you are reading when the moon is new or waning, what do you want to let go of (you can look at the fear and sorrow practice readings for ideas)?

The Stars: Experiment with astrology and navigate some potential plans or read to understand your relationships. See if you get impressions of times and circumstances with which to take action or with which to rest instead. Look into personality quirks that influence your professional and personal relationships.

INSIGHTS
Question or Focus (if any)

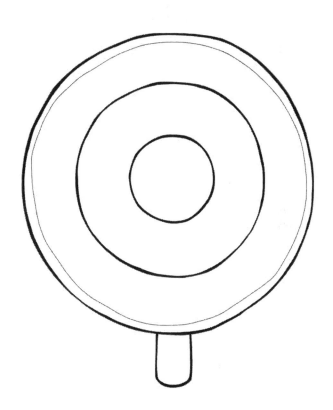

Practice 28:
READ FOR THE BASICS

Read for animals, letters, and shapes – see how many appear. An "s" shape can also look like a saxophone. An anchor or another clear symbol may be composed of smaller ones, such as small birds. Images can have two or three different possibilities.
 See how many basic symbols you can find. Possible categories include:

Animals
Buildings
Clothing
Faces
Furniture
Geometric Shapes
Letters of the Alphabet
Numbers
Plants
Spiritual Symbols
Zodiac Signs

Now see if these symbols have smaller symbols inside themselves.

Tip: *How do the images in the tea cup appear to communicate with each other? Do some images face each other? Is one image directly opposite another one on the other side of the cup?*

INSIGHTS
Question or Focus (if any)

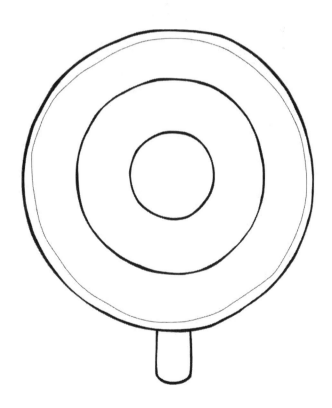

Practice 29:
READ "LIKE THE WIND"

Establish a theme or question for your reading. You may do a general reading, but read for a specific person or character with a clear living situation and set of intentions.

Quickly determine the images you see.

Quickly assess their story.

How did the images relate to each other?

Don't let yourself censor your interpretations. Let the thoughts swirl and shoot out. In other words, this is a "free write" using tea patterns as inspiration.

If you need structure, set a timer and spend two minutes looking at and writing about the images in each of the five sections: Bottom, Handle, Across, Middle, and Rim.

Tip: *Take pictures of your cup from various angles once the reading is prepared. This reduces concern over the leaves drying and falling, or shifting in any remaining liquid. It also allows for a different perspective on the images. Using the screen to examine the images can often inspire a quicker interpretation of the leaves than staring at the cup itself, especially in my experience when I began to read tea.*

INSIGHTS
Question or Focus (if any)

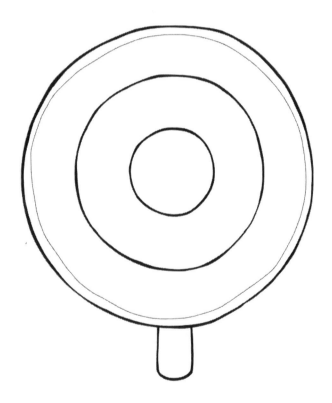

Practice 30:
READ TO HEAL OR COMFORT

This creative divination can become a nice gift to show you care about another person's recovery from an illness, accident, or other obstacle.

This exercise allows us to express and explore our instinct to help heal and take responsibility for someone else's health.

Tip: *It is ideal that you have the person's permission before doing this reading. Whenever you read for someone who isn't present, there is a risk of ethically compromising yourself and the other person. Respect privacy and free will.*

Bottom: How they may feel better
Handle: What they can do right now that is in their best interest
Across: What they can request from others
Middle: How they came to feel ill
Rim: Lessons to take away

Unfold this reading: Here's another method for finding comfort and healing. This method might help address chronic suffering as well as addiction.

Bottom: The nature of the problem
Handle: The responsibility of the person
Across: What is beyond the person's control
Middle: How they can negotiate their responsibilities and let go of what they wish to control
Rim: Other resolutions that could be considered

INSIGHTS
Question or Focus (if any)

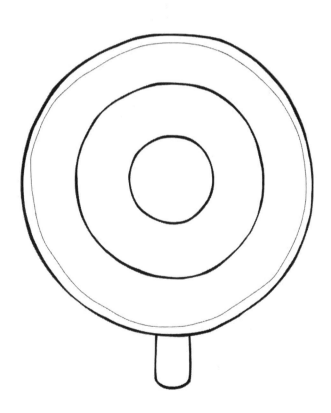

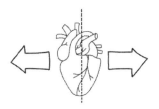

Practice 31:
RESOLVE OR AVOID CONFLICT

While no one can control the actions and thoughts of anyone else, creative divination is an often fruitful method for finding personal responsibility and resolutions.

Sometimes the strongest thing is letting go.

Sometimes the answers only come when you wait for them.

Many times problems fix themselves.

It's never the case you aren't needed. But are you taking on too much? Consider, as well – sometimes the most caring people forget to put themselves first.

Bottom: The real issue
Handle: What you/person being read can control
Across: How the other party, etc. views things, or any challenges you need to know about
Middle: Suggested resolutions
Rim: Possible immediate outcomes

Tip: *If leaves don't appear in helpful spots, always make the most of what does appear. Use this info. For example, what can you learn from the rooster at the bottom of the cup? How could pride or "ruling the roost" reflect on the situation? What can you learn from what you see throughout the cup?*

INSIGHTS
Question or Focus (if any)

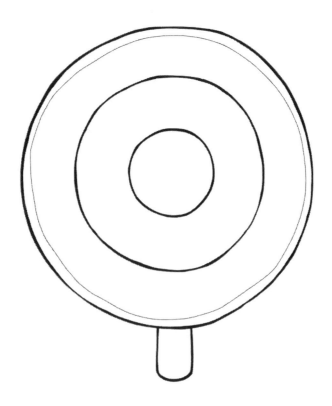

Practice 32:
INTERPRET RECURRING IMAGES IN DREAMS

Ask for more information on the themes and recurring images you have been pondering lately or have recently encountered.

Divide the cup in two parts. The first half will have the handle in the middle.

In the first half, look for: Clues about what the themes or images really are why you might be experiencing them or thinking about them right now.

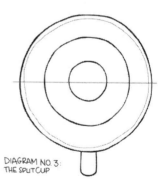

DIAGRAM NO. 3:
THE SPLIT CUP

In the second half, look for: Ideas about what the themes or images want you to know about yourself how to decide on what actions to take now.

Tip: *When doing a reading, write down your question before you begin. This helps focus the reading and keeps the answer from getting muddy or going off-base.*

INSIGHTS
Question or Focus (if any)

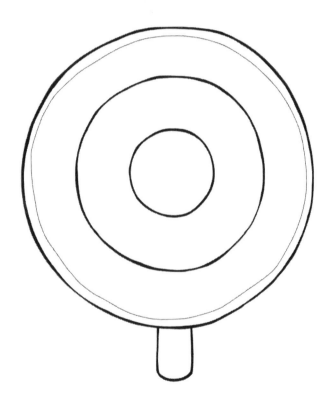

Practice 33:
WORK WITH YOUR SPIRIT ALLIES

Take this as an opportunity to communicate with any animal allies or spirit guides you feel you have. Or to get ideas on what they might be.

Bottom: The work you can do together (How you can connect)
Handle: What you can do for your spirit allies
Across: Who they are
Middle: Their messages for you
Rim: Possible outcomes

Unfold this reading: Try this reading once for each element, such as earth, air, fire, water, and spirit. See how spirit allies may communicate when you focus on those that work in each of these respective elements.

INSIGHTS
Question or Focus (if any)

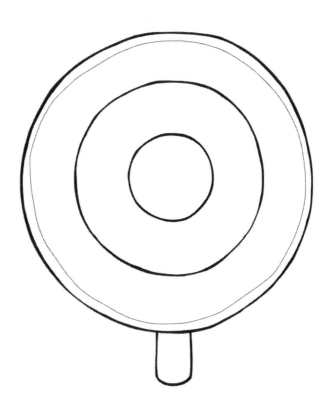

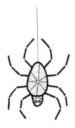

Practice 34:
RECOGNIZE THE GOOD YOU HAVE DONE

Recognizing one's ability to be generous, kind, and forgiving is an act to engage in periodically. Just as it is important to take stock of what might need pruning in your life, it is also rejuvenating to take a snapshot of what good acts, words, and ideas you bring into the world.

Bottom: Your good. How you have encouraged someone else, uplifted or helped someone in need, or how your daily work has benefited others
Handle: What good work can achieve – your current hopes for good work, or any thoughts you might have about good work
Across: Anything that could block good work, or the sacrifice of doing good work
Middle: How you have helped family, friends, or the community
Rim: How you can continue to commit small acts of kindness

Unfold this reading: What values represent your concept of goodness? Write or sketch your depiction of goodness that you want to embody. From this, pull 2-5.
Now **divide the cup into 2-5 sections**, depending on how many traits you selected. Read a

new cup of tea, where each section gives you more information about how to deepen your relationship with goodness in each of the facets of the concept that you have shared.

You can also create poetry, a story or song, a Venn diagram or bar graph using the 2-5 primary ideas of goodness that you have. Incorporate details from the tea leaf reading practice such as the amount of symbols in each section which can be applied to a diagram or bar graph.

Consider, too: How can you improve the world using this new piece of art? For example, were one of your qualities of goodness supporting charity or local businesses? How might this new creation be used to this end? Maybe it's as easy as sharing it on social media and raising awareness of a concept or organization that you feel resonates with you.

INSIGHTS
Question or Focus (if any)

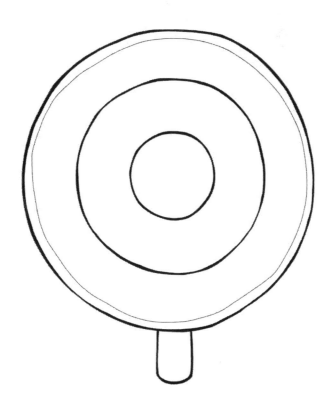

Practice 35:
HELP FORMULATE YOUR BRIGHT IDEA

This could, for example, be a business, organization, non-profit, or creative project, etc.

Bottom: Anything you need to know to help shape your idea
Handle: How to execute it
Across: What to manifest before you begin
Middle: How to formulate this new idea
Rim: When to launch this new idea

Tip: *Whenever you want a sense of a timeline for your new idea, you may divide the cup into fourths and read each section as either one week, if you want to know what to expect in the month ahead, or three months each, to get an idea of the year ahead.*

INSIGHTS
Question or Focus (if any)

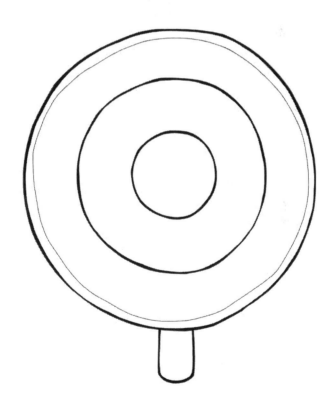

Practice 36:
READ FOR YOUR SHADOW SIDE

Our shadow side is that part of ourselves that is most primal, most hungry, and hidden in the shadows – because we are taught to believe that they are malicious or beastly.

While our shadow side is not "presentable", that basic self will aid us when we deal with it, and gnaw at us when we deny it.

Bottom: Details about your shadow – what you need to know, now

Handle: How your shadow works in your present day

Across: What you need to learn from this right now

Middle: How you and shadow work together

Rim: What you can leave behind, thanking shadow for this lesson

INSIGHTS
Question or Focus (if any)

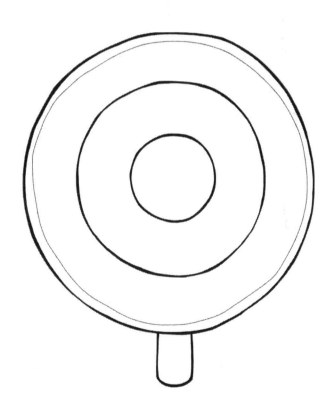

Practice 37:
ADAPT OR ADOPT TRAITS

What evolutionary traits (use of tools and technology, as well as changes in diet or routine) can you adapt to? What new things might be good for you to learn, now?

Bottom: Your potential for growth, or for welcoming something new into your life
Handle: What you can bring into your life to change and grow
Across: What's coming into your life that can be adapted to or adopted (you don't have to say yes)
Middle: Ideas for your next best steps
Rim: Any other ideas and tools you may need, and/or clarity on parts of the cup that may not have been clear

Tip: *Your eye may spot dragons in your tea cup. Or bunnies. Or dinos. I've seen all three quite often. If images are recurring, consider how they present the tools you need to take up. A dragon may offer quick and powerful transportation if well trained, but it could indicate a personal need to follow words of wisdom and let go of material comforts. A bunny might be a reminder to keep your senses keen for signs of danger, and rely on burrows and quick-thinking for safety. A dinosaur may mean it's time to honor the bones of a past that fascinates you, bury your worries, and even "play dead" around others.*

INSIGHTS
Question or Focus (if any)

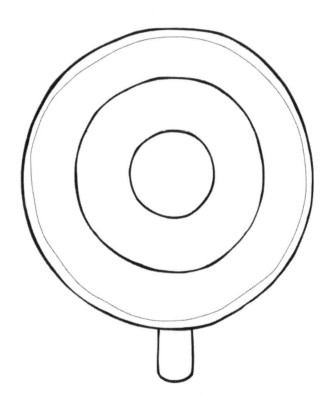

Practice 38:
RELEASE NEGATIVITY

We've all made mistakes. We all have ugly crap in our lives.

In order to become healthier people, it is useful to let go of some things. These may be material belongings. They may include emotional baggage. This could be anger or resentment, regret, or any other emotion that keeps you from fulfilling what you want.

Clean off the grime one day at a time so you shimmer as you are meant.

Bottom: Who you are, your essence
Handle: What you are ready to let go of
Across: The gifts of releasing it
Middle: Ideas for your next best steps – or who and what can help you let go
Rim: Any other solutions and tools you may need, and/or clarity on parts of the cup that may not have been clear

Unfold this reading: The images that you have seen during this creative divination exercise can be used to create anything (visual art, music, the written word, a performance) that allows you to let go.

You can choose to imagine solemnly burying each of the images or objects found in this reading, or whatever you have in your personal code of symbols that helps illustrate what you need to release.

You might want to visualize consciously burning them in a fire: Take your time building this fire in a meditation. Gather the materials, and picture yourself in a forest (or if the object itself is stationary, how could you imagine burning it down?).

You may set each object into a canoe and set it adrift on the river, stream, lake, or ocean.

You can also let the wind blow it all away.

However you choose to let go, the more detailed the experience, the more significant the outcome can be. What do your surroundings look, smell, taste, and feel like?

Repeat this visualization as often as needed.

Tip: *Ultimately it is up to you to continue the work of letting go of emotional baggage. But you can minimize the size of that mountain that blocks your sense of serenity through dedication to imagery or a ritual that uplifts you. This is the power of understanding your personal code, your language of the divine.*

INSIGHTS
Question or Focus (if any)

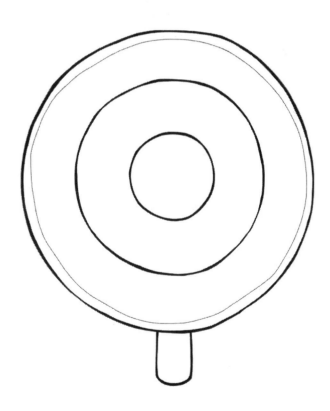

Practice 39:
SETTLE DOWN OR RELAX

Insomnia is something that many of us struggle with. It is also common for our minds to require a great deal of effort before they can relax.

Meditation and visualization exercises are popular methods to ease the body and settle the mind. Yoga and exercise are other options to help reduce tension and encourage a good night's sleep.

Like many methods of divination, this exercise allows you to look at some of the psychological and spiritual possibilities behind your current situation.

Bottom: What's bothering you, or why you cannot relax
Handle: What you can do about it now
Across: What you can do in the future
Middle: Things you should know about your goal to settle down
Rim: Further insights

Unfold this reading: Divide the cup in half. The first half will have the handle in the middle.

The first half represents what is keeping you awake. The other half represents what you can do to put yourself at ease.

INSIGHTS
Question or Focus (if any)

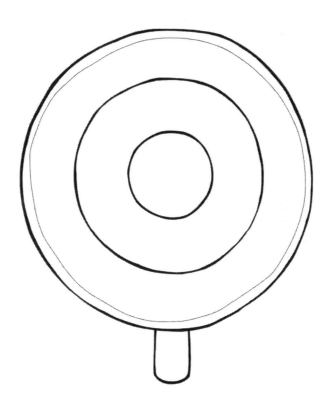

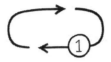

Practice 40:
GET A SONG OR PERSON OUT OF YOUR HEAD

Sometimes it is not just ourselves who are trapped in our head - often a song or person or a memory won't leave our brains.

Perhaps there is some creative reason that something keeps tapping into our membranes.

Bottom: Why the song, person, or memory is in your head
Handle: What you can do about it
Across: How you'll feel once it has cleared
Middle: The insights this song, person, or memory has to share with you
Rim: Clarity for anything unanswered

INSIGHTS
Question or Focus (if any)

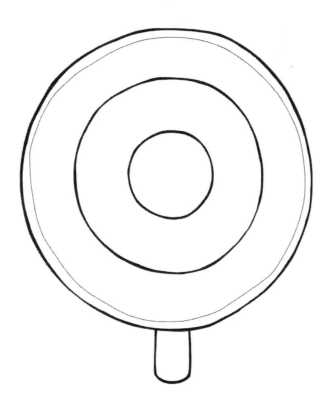

Practice 41:
BETTER KNOW YOUR NEIGHBOR(HOOD)

Who is next door to you? Or maybe, who is down the road, or the next island, boat, or cabin over? Maybe you do not know them well. Maybe you have vivid memories of people who lived next to you years ago, or next to someone you were close to.

Have them in mind for this reading.

Bottom: Your neighborhood
Handle: What you can share with your neighbor (new neighbors especially need information)
Across: What your new neighbor can show you
Middle: How you can expect to work together, and how you resolve conflicts
Rim: Your best course of action with your neighbor now

Unfold this Reading: How well do you know your neighborhood? Do you feel called to volunteer or be a better steward?

It's never too late to start something new.

Walk your neighborhood at least once a week. Visit your library. Spend an afternoon downtown or on Mainstreet. Support a local business. Make friends with a barista. Have a picnic in a park or nearby picturesque area.

Challenge yourself to explore places that are new to you. Learn more about buildings, birds, and plants around you. Ask friends and coworkers about their favorite restaurants and local experiences.

Maybe your new neighbor will come along.

INSIGHTS
Question or Focus (if any)

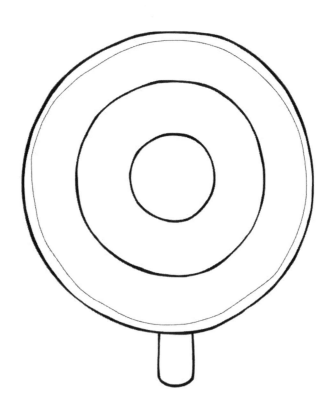

Practice 42:
SALUTE YOUR INNER WARRIOR

Imagine someone who has either agreed to a challenge and taken arms to fight for a greater cause, or someone who has faced personal difficulties head-on. Spiritual warrior or otherwise, they have seen the worst of some facet of this world. And they are ready for any insight from you and your tea leaves.

Maybe they want to know if they will find peace soon. Maybe the road ahead is long, and you will need to tell them.

Establish a very clear picture of your inner warrior. Detail what they look like. Include any distinguishing marks and characteristics on their skin color, hair, in their eyes, and how they carry themselves. Can you tell how old they are? Are they willing to talk about what they have recently accomplished or struggled with?

Bottom: Theme of the reading
Handle: The responsibilities of the inner warrior of the person being read
Across: Gifts, rewards, and challenges on the horizon
Middle: The present day
Rim: Possible outcome

Tip: *If you need inspiration, think of a time that you had to face something difficult. Do any images or colors, from what you wore or where you were, stand out? You can always imagine your inner warrior based on internet or library research.*

INSIGHTS
Question or Focus (if any)

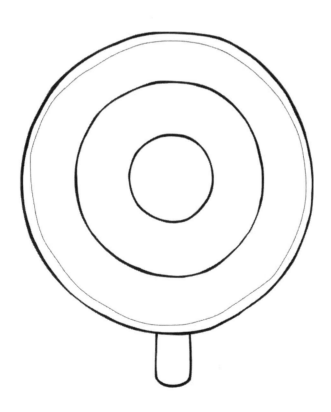

Practice 43:
IMPROVE ONE PART OF YOUR LIFE

If there was a prayer you could pray to help you better yourself for the benefit of others, what would that specialized prayer look like?

Use this practice reading when you have an area of your life that you want to make better.

Bottom: The theme of this area of life, and what it is teaching you now
Handle: What you can do now to improve it
Across: What you must let go of in yourself to improve
Middle: How you can look at things differently
Rim: Possible outcome

Tip: *The middle of the cup may reveal images that may illustrate how you can behave in a situation in a different way. A winged animal or a plane or helicopter may represent a need to rise above this particular part of your life. A walking cane can indicate that you need to accept assistance and support – it's ok to be humble.*

INSIGHTS
Question or Focus (if any)

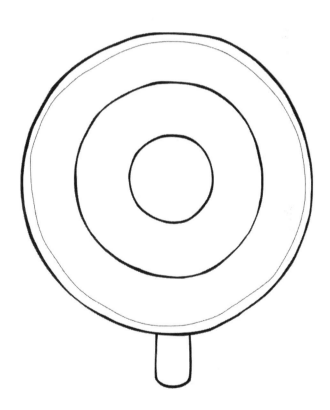

Practice 44:
COMMUNICATE WITH THE DEAD

In the quiet still of dreaming, I once heard a voice telling me to "get in touch with June". In about a month, my family and I had worked out what I instinctively recalled – my grandmother, who had passed away a year and a half before, had a close friend named June.

I called her, and continued to call her, off and on, for a couple of years. It was nice to reach out to someone who was a friend and contemporary of the woman who inspired me throughout my life.

And perhaps this was a message from my deceased grandmother.

Here's a creative divination practice that may help you tune in to those who have passed on.

Bottom: The identity of the dead
Handle: Your role in this communication
Across: The lens through which you might see this message
Middle: The message from the dead
Rim: Anything that needs to be clarified or highlighted

Tip: *Everyone has their own filter for how they view and express themselves. Consider contrasting your preconceptions with those of the person you may have identified in this reading.*

INSIGHTS
Question or Focus (if any)

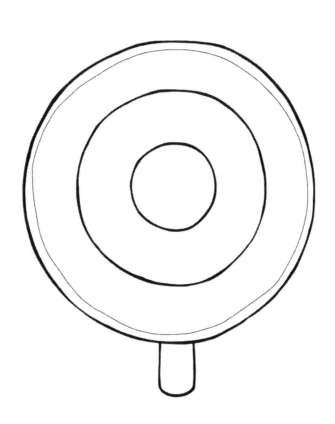

Practice 45:
UNDERSTAND YOUR FEARS

This reading helps you have a better grasp of your greatest fears, and can give you possibilities for overcoming them.

Not addressing your fears can only create larger monsters, and bring unhappiness to roost.

Bottom: The nature of my fears
Handle: The power I give to my fears
Across: The lesson my fears can teach me
Middle: What it is that I may be seeking that creates my fears
Rim: How to address my fears, as I understand them, now

INSIGHTS
Question or Focus (if any)

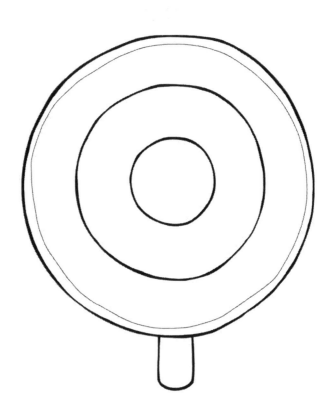

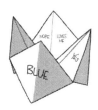

Practice 46:
UNDERSTAND YOUR LOVE INTERESTS

Whether you are in an established relationship with no desire to change, or you are crushing on someone who you are currently getting to know, this reading helps you see the bigger picture of your patterns.

Do you have a particular type of person you go for? What attracts you? What should you look out for?

Bottom: Your thoughts about your ideal love situation
Handle: What you bring to a relationship
Across: What you expect from your love interest
Middle: What you need to know about your love interest
Rim: Possible near future with this person

Unfold this reading: Try dividing your cup into four equal parts.

Each part answers a different question. One set of questions, for example, is:

Why am I attracted to this person?
What does this person feel about me?
Is this a healthy relationship?
How can I make the most of this situation?

INSIGHTS
Question or Focus (if any)

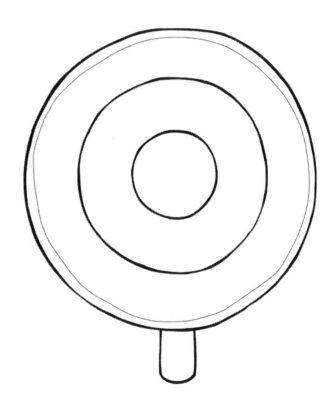

Practice 47:
YOUR FIVE YEAR PLAN

It helps to approach this reading with as simple a goal as possible. If you can pare down your goal to only one facet of your life, like "retirement" or "owning a house in the country", you will get the clearest results.

Not having a distinct focus for this reading will cause confusion, and it is likely that images relating to your main objective will appear in the leaves. These will give you a more expansive view of what is to come.

To help you get into the mood, *here is a **meditation***:

You are in a private, quiet area outdoors where you are free to meander through trees and bushes.

There is birdsong.

The weather and sounds are soothing.

You come to a comfortable bench in front of a fountain in the middle of a pond.

You sit on the bench, with a deep sense of serenity.

Imagine you see one of the people you looked up to as a child, who you cannot communicate with on this physical plane anymore, because of death, distance or time. This person is here to listen as you share something in common with them that you value within yourself.

Sit, talk about that mutual interest. Or simply give them your gratitude for showing up in this place of peace.

Begin the practice exercise.

Bottom: What to cultivate at this point in your life (for the next 1-5 years)
Handle: Who to spend time with
Across: Where to go
Middle: What to avoid doing
Rim: Possible outcomes

INSIGHTS
Question or Focus (if any)

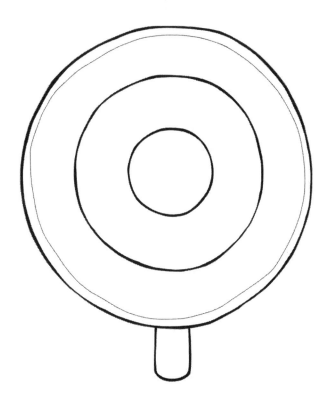

Practice 48:
READ FOR PEACE AND LOVE

You don't have to travel back to the Summer of Love to feel a sense of tranquility and understanding.

If you are seeking less complication and more healing and compassion, try this creative divination.

Begin by writing a "Peace and Love" letter. Describe what you mean by peace and love. Write about your vision of how you will feel, how you will act, and also how the people, animals, plants, and places in your world will communicate, feel, and act.

Tip: *Try to approach this reading by seeking peace and love in a small area of your life. This is desirable, as trying to change the entire world can be overwhelming for your energy and for your reading.*

Maybe you are more comfortable drawing your idea of peace and love. Or a mandala or a painting will express your concept.

Bottom: Where you can find peace and love
Handle: How you create your own peace and love
Across: How you give peace and love
Middle: The sacrifices needed for peace and love
Rim: Possible outcomes

INSIGHTS
Question or Focus (if any)

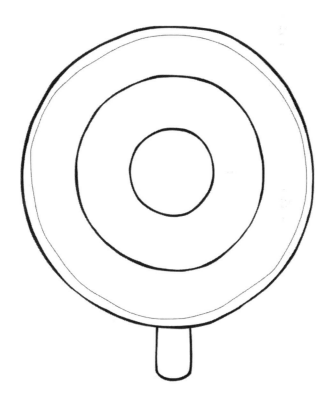

Practice 49:
READ FOR PROTECTION

Energy vampires, harsh critics, bad vibes in your immediate environment, a tough home or work situation, can all give us a need for protection. And whether we are highly sensitive or not, anything that might make local, national, or global headlines can concern us, shake us, even bring us to tears.

Here is a suggested reading for protection. A simple stick-like leaf could be a **wand** or a **pen**. **Letters** might indicate a community you can rely on:

Bottom: Sword and shield (What can you take up to defend and protect yourself?)
Handle: Drawbridge (How can you choose to allow energy to affect you?)
Across: Sentinels (How can your support groups look out for you?)
Middle: Kingdom (What do you cherish about yourself?)
Rim: Messengers (What do you need to be aware of?)

Tip: *Trust the process of creating and reigniting your personal code. The walls and armor we build to protect ourselves can benefit as well as harm. And they are highly individualized. Expect unique imagery.*

INSIGHTS
Question or Focus (if any)

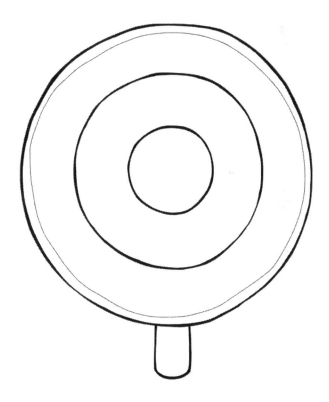

Practice 50:
READ FOR BETTER HEALTH

One of the hardest things to do a psychic reading for, in my opinion, is better health. Even if one's aim is as common as weight loss, it is still difficult – even ill-advised – to give advice.

Psychics are not doctors (or lawyers or other professionals, with some exceptions).

Tea leaves and an exploration of one's imagination both can lead to creative ideas for how to improve one's physical or mental health.

While understanding that readings, and this creative divination, are no replacement for the advice of a professional, there is no reason this cannot be used as an entertaining supplement.

Bottom: Possible source of your genuine health concern
Handle: What you have been doing for your health
Across: Resources you may need to consider
Middle: What better health looks like in your near future
Rim: Anything you need to know

INSIGHTS
Question or Focus (if any)

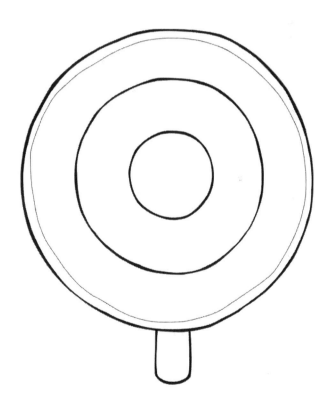

Practice 51:
READ FOR MOTHER AND CHILD

This reading regards mothers of all stripes. It is primarily inspired by my close friend Kellie Barr and her experiences with pregnancy and raising children. It is adaptable to the practice of honoring mothers (and parents!) of anyone or anything: creative projects, animals, causes, communities, and more.

*Begin with this **meditation:***

Imagine you are in your mother's womb.
Listen for her heartbeat.
Breathe in, filling your stomach, by the count of four.
Hold your breath for four counts.
Breathe out, by the count of four.
Leave your lungs empty for the count of four.
Listen again for her heartbeat. Thank her for her connection to you.
What does her smile look like? What do her hands feel like? How do her kisses feel on your cheek when you are young?
Repeat the breathing technique.

Look for the pulse of the child you are going to give birth to or have given birth to. Seek it out with your intuition.

What makes your child smile? What are their hands doing when they offer healing and love? How do they express themselves at their best?

Repeat the breathing pattern.

Take what time you need to honor this space and meditation.

Open your eyes when you are ready.

Feel free to write down anything you experienced during this meditation that you find worth noting. Also, you may wish to write down and answer these questions: What makes me smile? What do my hands do when I offer healing and love? How do I express myself at my best?

When you look at your cup, here are ways to examine the leaves and their positions.

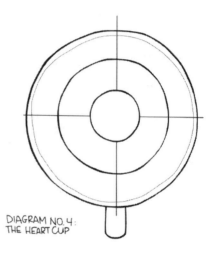

DIAGRAM NO. 4:
THE HEART CUP

Lower Left: What your child is here to help you learn
Upper Left:: How you can help your child as their student
Upper Right: Anything they need you to know
Lower Right: What you can look forward to in your relationship
Bottom: How you can help your child as a mother

INSIGHTS
Question or Focus (if any)

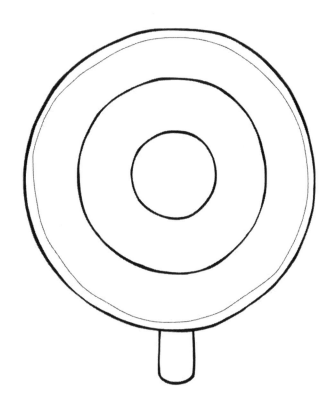

Practice 52:
READ TO INTERPRET NEGATIVE SPACE

You may have noticed in your practice readings that negative space generates shapes, letters, numbers, animals, and more. In other words, the empty spaces in between the tea leaves also create images.

The image of a house relies often on negative space. It gives it the impression of a roof or the front wall or a door.

Perform a practice reading where you focus on what appears in the spaces between the leaves.

You may find the leaves themselves are more clear than the space that lies between them. The leaves often remain more interesting. Don't ignore all that information, but gather it and record it. Use the leaves as well as the negative spaces.

Find and write about at least three negative spaces - maybe they all appear like nonsense, and that's ok.

INSIGHTS
Question or Focus (if any)

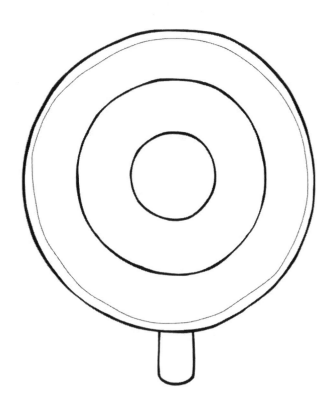

Practice 53:
COUNTERPARTS AND OPPOSITES

For example, you find a mermaid in your tea leaves. And an acorn. And a fence. And a tie someone would wear for a formal occasion.

What do these symbols offer when you flip them on their heads and determine their opposite symbol?

After recording your tea leaf reading, tracking its symbols and letting your intuition and imagination swirl around with possibilities and stories, *write two lists.*

Take a few symbols that puzzle you most. Or that you most strongly identify with. Or list everything!

Write one list dedicated to opposites and the other for counterparts. Go with your first, most immediate response. For example:

Counterparts: **mermaid – sailor**
acorn – tree
fence – ditch
tie – chest

Tip: *Interpreting the meaning of a symbol involves thinking of how it relates to something it often works with or alongside. For example, how a tie is worn over the chest.*

Opposites: mermaid – **crone in a desert**
acorn – **feather**
fence – **cloud**
tie – **bare feet**

Have fun with this exercise. You should see how your psyche works to give you insights into your personality and how your brain works.

INSIGHTS
Question or Focus (if any)

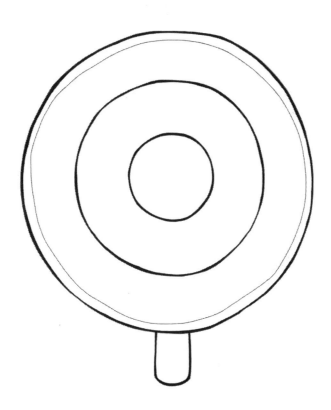

PART TWO: Reading AS

These practice readings particularly allow you to explore all the possible archetypes within and without you.

Open your imaginary wardrobe, access the costumes and makeup that might be called for along the way. Dress up or dress down or, in some cases, you may feel as naked as can be.

These readings allow you to be someone else.

Practice 54:
YOUR DESTINY SELF

As Nancy Antenucci, author of *The Psychic Tarot Book*, wrote in a lesson she designed on Embodied Divination:

"Imagine yourself on the last day of your life, an older version of yourself who has completely manifested this life's destiny. Listen quietly as this future self appears. Ask this future self what you need to be on your path of authentic living or what may be needed to change your current direction."

Imagine the tea leaf reading is your opportunity to see anything you wish from the eyes of your destiny self.

Tip: *If whatever you hoped for in a reading are not easy to intuit or imagine when you first record the images, brainstorm on them after the reading. This doesn't have to happen in the same sitting, it can be up to a month later, though no more than one week is recommended.*

INSIGHTS
Question or Focus (if any)

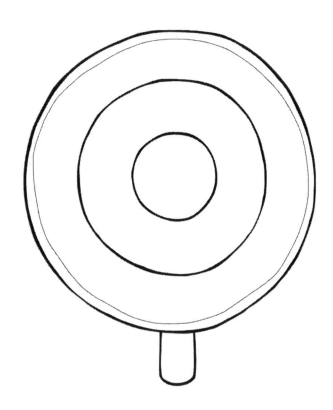

Practice 55:
A MAGICAL CHILD

The concept of the Magical Child is one of the archetype options available within the four archetypes of survival shared and studied by Caroline Myss. Her book *Sacred Contracts* goes into greater length.

The Magical Child believes nothing is impossible, and comes from a place of innocence.

As you do this creative divination, consider a mindset that exists in possibility, and let your mind play with the images you find.

For a little structure, use the locations described in the next creative divination exercise.

INSIGHTS
Question or Focus (if any)

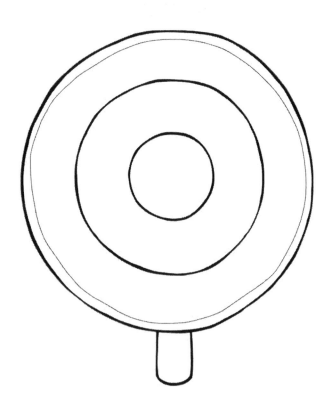

Practice 56:
A FIGURE IN MYTH

Find a mythological figure – one rooted in a culture that is at least a few generations old. It can be from a creation myth. Or a destruction myth.

You may wish to write, meditate, or create art to understand where this mythological figure and you might relate to each other (it could be Persephone, or the Minotaur, or Hephaestus, or Psyche, or Medusa, or anyone outside of Greek mythology).

Try using the **bottom of the cup** to find images of where you relate to this figure.

Try using the **middle of the cup** to search for images that this figure in myth understands as their present day – or *the* present state of affairs, on a larger scale that applies to your community or a larger matter, like a scientific breakthrough or a political concern.

Try using **the rim** to predict the next step, or the next stage.

If you feel stuck, think about the myth that your mythological figure is a part of. Are there any elements or tools in there that may also be hidden in the cup? You can also find another myth to consider. You can also use this practice reading to discover connections in myths that may be helpful to you or someone else.

Tip: *Instinct first, research later. If you feel overwhelmed by the task of interpreting symbols, and this exercise feels especially complex, refer to a symbol dictionary or book on animal meanings, as appropriate. You are welcome to research shapes and their standard meanings. And in this case, an understanding of a mythological figure on a greater level is helpful. But start with what you know you know, or your first impressions. They are powerful and they are the core of your personal code.*

INSIGHTS
Question or Focus (if any)

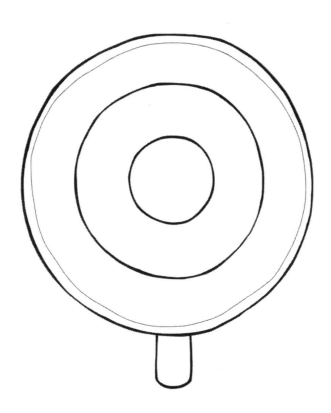

Practice 57:
A SHAPESHIFTER

You can read as a nondescript shapeshifter: A person or animal that turns into one, or multiple creatures. Or you can put on the persona of Professor Lupin from the Wizarding World of Harry Potter. Maybe try on the mindset of a vampire known to turn to a bat. Imagine you can turn into an owl or crow or peacock.

The key is to walk between two worlds, use that framework. You can make up your own shapeshifting persona, if werewolves and vampires, and so on don't call to you.

Now look at the cup with the eyes of this shapeshifter. **Divide the cup into two**, and view one side from one of the shapeshifter's realities and the other from the second reality (human vs werewolf, for example).

What do they see, knowing that they view nature with much more intimate detail than most

DIAGRAM NO. 3:
THE SPLIT CUP

people? What meaning do they apply to shapes that look like plants, trees, animals, and clouds? Are they at the mercy of these images, or are they powerful allies?

How can you relate to this shapeshifter after this reading? How do you share their strengths? What weaknesses can you empathize with?

INSIGHTS
Question or Focus (if any)

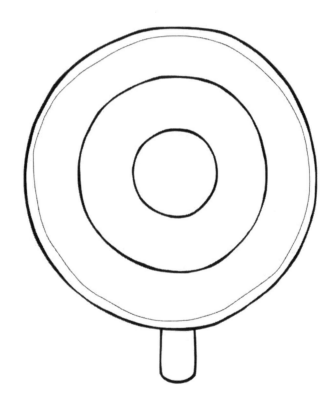

Practice 58:
THE PERSON WHO TAUGHT YOU COMPASSION

While it may be difficult to pinpoint one person who taught you about compassion, you may recall a few times in your life where you learned a lesson in compassion. Someone showed what it meant to be compassionate to someone else, or told you how important it was to greet others with a smile and a hello. Perhaps you learned what it felt like to be treated with compassion.

Tip: *This is a helpful creative divination to do for someone you have a resentment toward. This person could be a parent or other relative, a spouse or partner, a co-worker, a school mate, or a part of yourself.*

Imagine that person needs insight from this exercise. See compassionately into the tea leaves for an idea on how you might help. Remember, with resentments, that both parties are suffering.

If you have a clear concept of someone who taught you compassion, concentrate on the solutions they would find within the images.

An object that may look like a **nest** or a **broken tree branch** would symbolize my grandfather in my personal code. After a windstorm took down a nest of hatchlings, he was convinced my brother and I could care for them.

A **rake** or **snake** or **box** would bring to mind my father and the time he transported a large garden snake from the backyard to a nearby field. A **spider** might evoke something similar for you. A **bowl, plate**, or other **kitchen objects** and **food items** would indicate sharing and nourishment.

INSIGHTS
Question or Focus (if any)

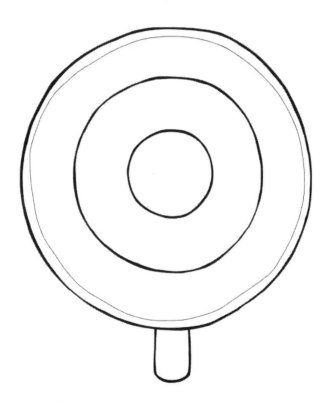

Practice 59:
THE PERSON WHO CHALLENGES YOU MOST

This creative divination can be done for two types of people: A person who challenges you most may challenge you in seemingly negative ways – making you feel less-than, perhaps resisting your goals or disagreeing with your objectives and values. Or perhaps they inspire you – you admire their successes, and maybe they are even in a teacher or mentor role in your life, where you are often pushed to improve yourself.

List five of the things that you think really motivate this person to challenge you in the way that they do.

Now, imagine those items as different senses: Seeing, hearing, touching, feeling, and tasting.

Once you feel you have entered the world of this person who challenges you, once you almost feel you can sense things through their body, begin this creative divination and interpret what your challenging person sees, hears, touches, feels, and tastes.

INSIGHTS
Question or Focus (if any)

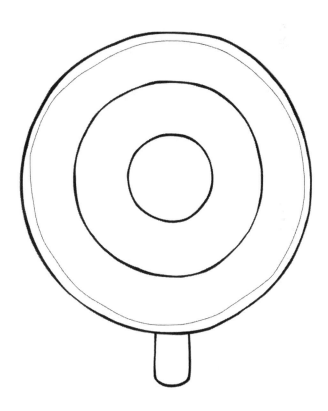

Practice 60:
THE PERSON WHO BROKE YOUR HEART

This creative divination may be the hardest one, or the one most emotionally traumatic.

Perhaps you glorify a past love and mistake their hard edges for attractive traits. Or you have easily forgotten the disagreements and shortcomings of a different partner.

Attempting to find empathy for this other person, before concentrating on the details of their personality and worldview, will help guide this exercise (and more importantly, you as you do it).

Begin with compassion – What was their childhood like? How involved were their parents? What were their values? What pastimes did you share? What did they enjoying doing that you do not care for at all?

Adopt their type of language and vision for this creative divination. Give images a second look after you have initially listed them.

Perhaps their love of **crystals** or **cars** or **bicycles** or **goats** will appear in tea leaves that at first didn't resemble a **polished stone** or a **hubcap** or a **bike path** or a **jumping goat**.

INSIGHTS
Question or Focus (if any)

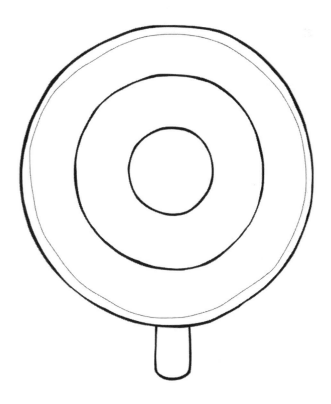

Practice 61:
YOUR HERO(INE)

This can be:
- a political hero(ine)
- someone from fiction, fantasy, or comic books or any entertainment media
- someone that you aspire to be like
- a personal connection
- someone from your past

You may choose to return to this practice reading and try out all of these possible personas.

Tip: *Use this creative divination when you are in the midst of change and opportunity.*

Unfold this reading: Think of a hero(ine) who can assist you with a challenge you must face. Have you lost a job or need to move or sell a home? Who would provide a good model for how to go forward?

Consider their experiences and how they handle their situations. Let that guide your intuition and imagination as you read the tea leaves.

INSIGHTS
Question or Focus (if any)

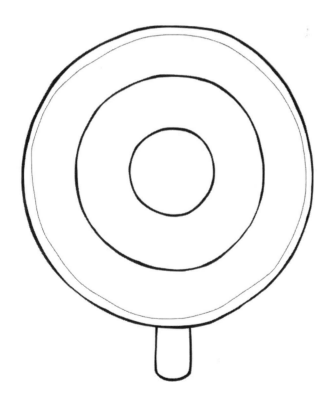

Practice 62:
A TAROT COURT CARD

There are 16 tarot court cards. Many decks assign various titles to them, and the rather common Rider-Waite-Smith tradition refers to them as pages, knights, queens, and kings. There is one of each of these personas for each of the four suits, or four elements: swords (air), wands (fire), cups (water), and pentacles (earth).

You may choose to look up a tarot court card image online for inspiration. You can select a card either by drawing one at random from a shuffled tarot deck, or by selecting one based on the Myers-Briggs correlations shared here.

If you don't know your Myers-Briggs personality type, take a Myers-Briggs quiz, easily found online:

ISTP- Page of Coins   ESTP- Knight of Coins
INFP- Page of Cups   ENFP- Knight of Cups
ISFP-Page of Wands   ESFP- Knight of Wands
INTP- Page of Swords   ENTP- Knight of Swords
ISTJ- Queen of Coins   ESTJ- King of Coins
INFJ- Queen of Cups   ENFJ- King of Cups
ISFJ- Queen of Wands   ESFJ- King of Wands
INTJ- Queen of Swords   ENTJ- King of Swords

Consider the court card personality's place in the world seen on its card. What are its roles? How does it see its world?

Picture doing this creative divination as the person in the card in the moment illustrated on it.

Tip: *Tea reading, tarot, Myers-Briggs, and disciplines like runes and astrology may seem daunting when they are new. But you already know a lot about them.*

*Fire personalities (wands)
are often passionate.*

*Water personalities (cups)
are more emotional.*

*Air personalities (swords)
are more mental.*

*Earth personalities (pentacles)
are often detail-oriented.*

Unfold this reading: Imagine you are the same tarot court card, or a new one. Now imagine it gets to have a few secret minutes in the role of another court personality in the deck. Sit or stand for a moment on a knight's horse, or a king or queen's throne, or in the landscape of one of the pages.

How is this point of view different? How do these new responsibilities influence how this personality interprets their tea leaves? How has their own sense of space and their own environment changed?

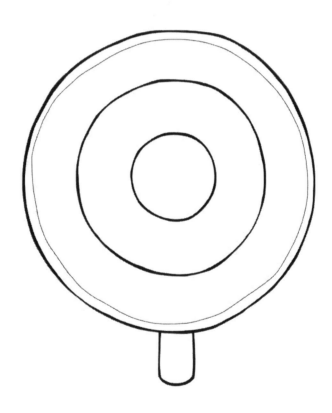

INSIGHTS
Question or Focus (if any)

Practice 63:
A FAVORITE CARTOON CHARACTER

A cartoon character does not have to be bouncy or happy.

Animated characters can often bend their environments to their will. Or they help depict common feelings, thoughts, or struggles we face.

Tip: *With creative divination, anything can happen. You can do the unexpected – if you're flattened out by life, here's how you can unflatten yourself.*

If you don't have a modern cartoon character you relate to, consider the cartoons you watched growing up. Did you collect a lot of things with that character on them? Was a Roadrunner sleeping bag something you hoped Santa would bring you?

Bottom: What the character wants to bring to your attention
Handle: How you are like this character
Across: What this character would do in your situation
Middle: The possibilities of doing one new thing as if you were this character at this time
Rim: Unexpected information

INSIGHTS
Question or Focus (if any)

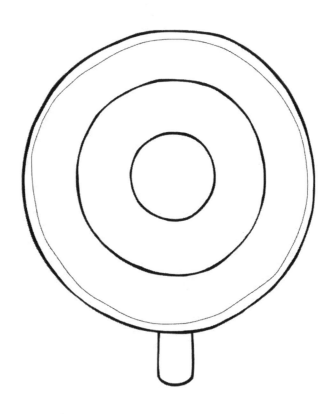

Practice 64:
A FORCE OF NATURE

What if you were the wind, or a tsunami, or a snowstorm? Be a volcano, a tornado, an earthquake, a flood. A wildfire. *How do you see yourself making changes?*

How would you approach perceiving the images in the tea? Would you whip around the cup? Would you easily touch ground? Would you change as tedious as a glacier?

Tip: *This may be the easiest way to begin reading tea leaves. It's not you. You don't even come from a human place. You either come to the reading with all sorts of built up momentum and energy, or you may gradually bury the experience with your "snow" or "rain".*

In fact, a slow process of unfolding the meaning in a tea leaf reading is very natural, and almost necessary, especially as time progresses. Your skills need to develop. Wherever your abilities are.

Mary K Greer, in *Tarot for Your Self,* advises returning to the same tarot card reading six months after a reading, and then one year after the original reading, too. She advocates honoring readings done for milestones, like a birthday or a favorite personal or public holiday, in particular: These are more distinct for your mind and emotions.

By turning back to the same reading after a set period of time, you aren't only like the weather, seasonally revisiting the same landscape. You also give yourself a chance to comprehend the symbols and patterns that create a core truth for yourself. And you can take this understanding of particular symbols and patterns and later apply it to readings done for others.

Because you, dear, are a force of nature. How do you see yourself making changes?

INSIGHTS
Question or Focus (if any)

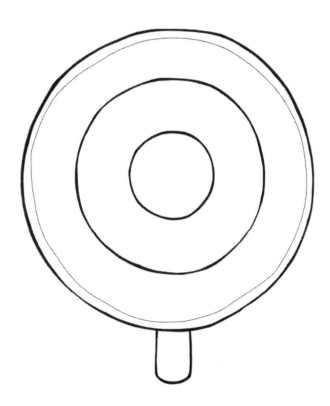

Practice 65:
READ AS A TITAN

It's a major job parenting the Olympic gods and goddesses. It does not get any bigger.

Unless you're Uranus and Gaea, but no one's here to put the pressure of being the Earth and Sky on you.

Do try reading as if you are the Alpha, the beginning of energies. Everything is new. Everything cries for a name.

This might be a perfect way to describe how you feel when you first approach reading tea leaves.

What on earth is all this in the cup? What's this junk? You may rightly ask.

If you're a Titan looking at it, your perspective isn't wrapped up in your modern view. Nope. You're just huge, primal power, and the universe is up for grabs. Really! Saturn, you may recall, is named after the leader of the Titans.

I encourage you to research the stories of the Titans, or review them if you are already familiar. There's some wonderful depth in those archetypes!

Essentially, try reading tea leaves as if you were the beginning of the energy of memory (this is where all inspiration comes from), or the energy of the oceans, or the energy of the sun and light, or the energy of justice and order, or the energy of rivers.

Remember this is ancient energy. And that this energy may also come from a prototype clever mother who saves her children by outsmarting her male counterpart.

INSIGHTS
Question or Focus (if any)

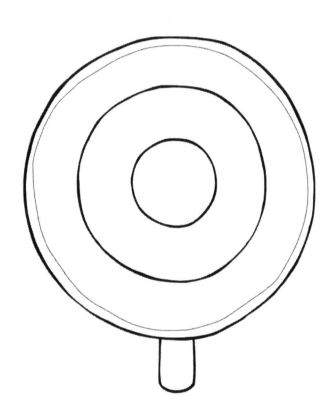

Practice 66:
A MUSE

Your job, as a muse, is to find ways to inspire someone.

This person might be down on their luck, broken hearted, or an artist primed for their next project. Maybe you will read for a person who needs to recognize their talents!

In many ways, your clients, whether they know it or not, are inspired by your behavior and insight as a reader. As a creative diviner, you *are* a muse.

First, determine what sort of muse you want to read as. You can encourage dance, art, theatre, comedy, history, the sciences, writing, music, or romantic gestures! Be more particular than this, even, if you want to inspire a scrapbooker, dressmaker, or poet in grad school.

Second, who is your seeker? Do you imagine someone who is overworked but loves to sing or do watercolor? Someone who finds time, always, for learning about a particular interest, and wants to either share that with others, or continue their studies?

Both of these frameworks help you approach any divination in a direct, clear regard.

Yes, you can be both seeker and reader. No, you don't need to be terribly specific in either respect, regarding the "art" you must inspire: Making spaghetti or toast is an artform. Cleaning house is an act where muses tread, too.

Tip: *Don't be afraid to think big or work small. Read towards what is comfortable for you.*

INSIGHTS
Question or Focus (if any)

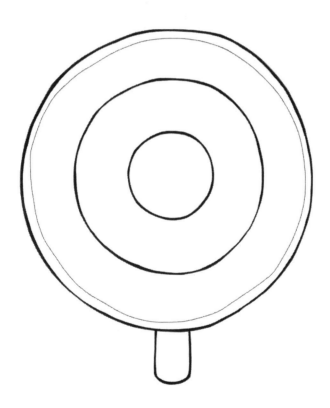

Practice 67:
A DIFFERENT ENVIRONMENT

What if you read as someone who lived near a river? Or on a mountain? Or deep inside the ocean? Or on the moon? Or in orbit around Saturn?

Curl up inside your proverbial cabin in the woods. Choose a place that you feel you could do meditative work from. Somewhere there is peace, or at the very least, permission for you to relax and have the space to observe small and large scale information.

Because this information feed gets to filter the reading you do next.

Pick your new environment (it can be fictional, too, like a favorite place in a cartoon or a myth or a movie or tv series).

Then, you may wish to center yourself and try this **meditation to visualize this environment,** *to help your mind click into place, before you begin:*

Close your eyes. Should any sounds distract you, try to translate them into sounds that might be natural to the new environment you have decided to step into for this divination practice.

Are there birds? Babbling brooks? The washing weight of the ocean?

You are walking down stairs to a long hallway full of doors.

At the end of this hallway is one door. This door leads to your new environment.

You are in no hurry to reach it, but as you draw closer, the sounds of that environment grow gradually louder.

You can also see what this door looks like.

How does the frame of it look? What color is it? What material is it made of?

What shape is it? How sturdy or thick is it?

How does it open? Can you slide it, push it, or pull it? And what does the knob or latch look like or feel like?

When you are ready, open the door.

Step inside.

You see a private space for yourself in this environment. The door closes behind you and you reach your sanctuary, observing any plants, animals, cosmos, colors and textures along the way.

Settle into your environment.

When you are ready, begin your reading.

INSIGHTS
Question or Focus (if any)

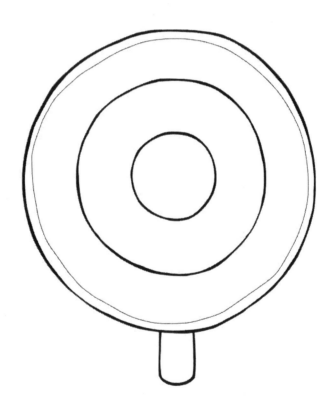

Practice 68:
A STUDENT

You are here to discover, to take notes, to ask questions.

Let's argue there are three phases of a typical student in a semester: At the beginning, this student may be anxious, but is primarily determined to get a decent grade. At the middle of the semester, there may be some resentment or guilt about how their class is going (this isn't always completely the student's fault!). Come finals, the pressure is on: And. It. Is. Crunchtime!

The heat is on.

Tip: *Neither creativity or divination are about having all the absolute answers. You don't have to know all the answers, and there is no right or wrong.*

Time yourself – 20 minutes – to see how much you can get from your cup of tea. This is time from finishing the tea and taking down your first impressions on the template to being able to hand in your finished final.

Your complete final includes:

- At least three-five distinct images in the tea (A **squirrel** viewed from left to right can definitely look like a **scorpion** viewed from right to left. That works as two of the three images.).
- A representation of their size and where they sit in the cup, on the template.
- A five word to one-sentence personal code definition of each image – what it represents.
- One brief paragraph each on how each symbol applies to the person being read and their situation.

INSIGHTS
Question or Focus (if any)

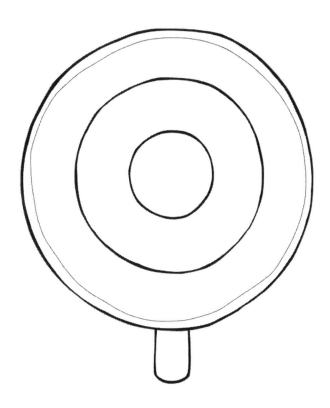

Practice 69:
A SPY OR DETECTIVE

How would a sleuth or a secret operative see their tea leaves? A tea leaf reading is a perfect method to examine possible patterns and investigate and deduce where things may be heading.

In this practice reading, look at the cup to answer:

How might the leaves in the cup be seen as victims of crime or as potential targets or allies?

What are the strategies illustrated in the cup?

Sort out the sequence of events. Work to decipher the clues of this moment in time.

Tip: *Pay attention to the body language within the images in your cup. Does it appear as if creatures and human beings are looking in a given direction? Do one of their limbs, or a tail give away their interest? What does that particular hand or paw, finger or claw, symbolize? Are the figures alert or relaxed? Are all the images whole or are they broken or compromised by other images?*

INSIGHTS
Question or Focus (if any)

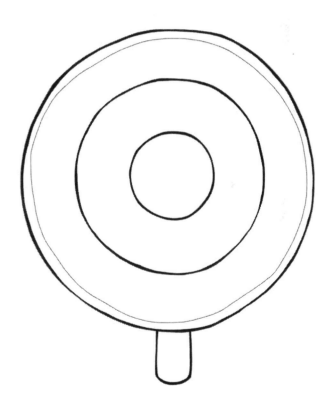

Practice 70:
SOMEONE WHO SAW HER STANDING THERE

Your gut does acrobatics every time you see the object of your affection: A person, a place, a being, an object, a part of yourself.

Dance, now, with that object of your desire. Imagine you are reading your cup as if it is this person you adore.

Every detail is intriguing. You want to know as much as possible about it.

And everything is so great, yes? Maybe it's *not* all "yes". Maybe some of it is "no".

Read this cup with the enthusiasm of someone who has found someone new, lively, and attractive to flirt with. Welcome all possibilities.

Read for 5-10 minutes with this open-hearted enthusiasm.

Then, spend 3-5 minutes looking again at the cup.

Find as many red flags as you can – as many reasons as possible that this same person or situation is *not* beneficial for you.

How is the information in the cup showing you potential danger or disaster?

Be honest. It can save you (and what you desire) many troubles.

INSIGHTS
Question or Focus (if any)

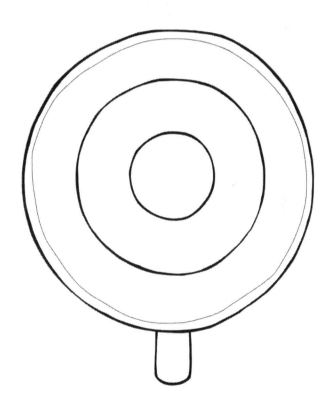

Practice 71:
THE GRADUATE

Congratulations.

You're off and on your way to begin the next phase of your life. It's your time to begin really getting to know yourself outside of your immediate family or the community you've known as a student. Regardless what level of schooling, there's always a core family that cannot be brought with you after your education concludes.

It may be that you're done with specific training or a degree, and entering the working world to the best of your capabilities.

It's a bold transition.

Look into your tea cup for signs of how you or the person being read takes new action.

Bottom: Goal or theme for this snapshot in time
Handle: The parts of yourself you must take with you
Across: The people and resources you have now that will remain of most value to you
Middle: Patterns to be aware of
Rim: Possibilities in the future

INSIGHTS
Question or Focus (if any)

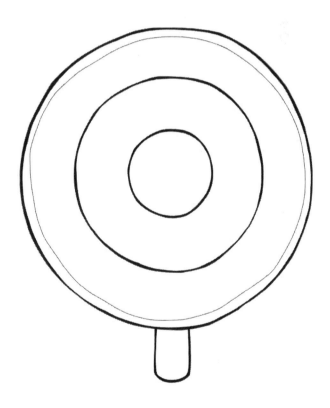

Practice 72:
THE BIRTHDAY KID

You may know someone who has a birthday soon. Whether living, deceased, easy to contact, or estranged, consider reading for them. Picture that person in your mind.

Or choose someone who was born the same week – or the same day – as you! It could be Chopin or George Washington or George Harrison.

Bottom: Birthday kid's expectations for the year ahead
Handle: Birthday kid's genuine needs this year
Across: The big lessons for the birthday kid right now
Middle: Allies who are with the birthday kid and any messages they have
Rim: Possible outcome or nature of the birthday kid's wish

INSIGHTS
Question or Focus (if any)

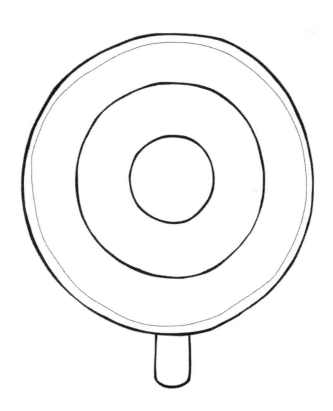

Practice 73:
WHAT'S IN A NAME?

Try reading for someone who either shares your first, last, or middle name, has a similar name, or shares your initials. This can either be someone from a fictional world or someone famous.

For example, your middle name might be shared by a member of your family.

You may either ask them what they would like a reading about, or tap into their personality and let that be your guide.

Tip: *Before any reading, it is good practice to establish what the person being read wants to walk away with. What do they want from their experience? Peace of mind on an area of their life? Reassurance on a decision they made? Advice? Or simply general input?*

INSIGHTS
Question or Focus (if any)

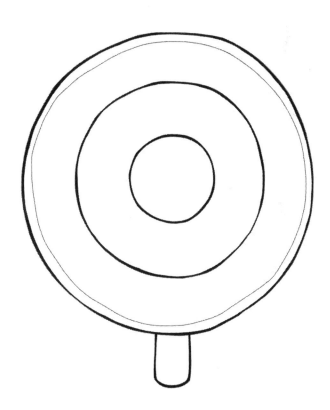

Practice 74:
A FAVORITE BOOK CHARACTER

Reunite with a character from a book you loved years and years ago, as a child or as an adult. Or choose someone or something you've encountered in one of the more recent books you've read or listened to.

Imagine you have their best and worst traits. Impersonate their voice and/or mannerisms. Maybe do a little - or a lot! - of cosplay.

Set a special space up for your tea leaf reading that might echo their own natural habitat. Perhaps you can even use their favorite tea for this practice reading.

Bottom: What your character wants the person being read to know

Handle: How your character might share this message

Across: How their message may be received

Middle: The present situation between the character and the person being read

Rim: Future possibilities for the person being read, based on what their reader shared with them

INSIGHTS
Question or Focus (if any)

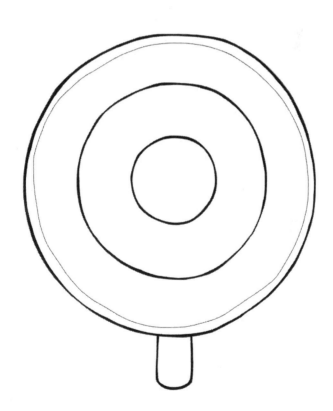

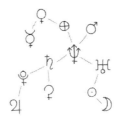

Practice 75:
USE ASTROLOGY

Let the stars help shape your story. You can:

• Look for constellations in your tea cup, and incorporate the tales behind them.
• Look for insight based on astrological influences at the present moment.
• Try a relationship reading – **divide the cup in half from the handle up** and choose each side to represent one person and their astrological influences. Dividing it in this manner indicates that both people in the relationship have responsibilities, because the handle is in both sections.
• Help set goals: If there is something you wish to accomplish or are curious about in the future, learn what you can from an astrologer – or simply search online. Take information about where the planets are and hold that concept in mind as you do a reading focused on that future time and your intentions.

INSIGHTS
Question or Focus (if any)

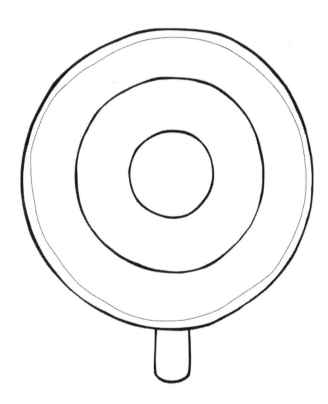

Practice 76 to 78:
READ THE SERENITY PRAYER

You may, for this one, use one cup and read for the insight throughout this simple prayer.
I think that each element of the prayer can be worth its own reading:

"God, grant me the serenity
to accept the things I cannot change,"

Bottom: What serenity has – or has not – looked like to you in the past
Handle: Your role in serenity
Across: Anything you need to know about serenity
Middle: How you can gain serenity now
Rim: Future gifts from working on your serenity throughout your life

"the courage to change the things I can,"

Bottom: What courage means to you
Handle: How you can be courageous now (if empty, maybe you do not need to act courageously, or need to think of yourself as courageous – you already are)
Across: Anything you need to know about changing things in your life
Middle: How you can gain courage now
Rim: Future gifts from working on transformation throughout your life

For possible suggestions on what you might choose to be change in your life, try practice readings 6, 8, or 13.

"and the wisdom to know the difference."

Bottom: What the wisdom to discern has – or has not – looked like to you in the past
Handle: Your role in being discerning
Across: Anything you need to know about acceptance and courage
Middle: How you can gain wisdom now
Rim: Future gifts from working on your ability to be accepting of things you cannot change as well as unafraid of changing what you can throughout your life

Tip: *Grounding yourself for a reading is not only good practice, but can prepare participants to accept their experience. The prayer I speak for my readings: "We ask that higher power and the universe help guide this reading, and give (person being read) the courage to do with this experience what is appropriate for them at this time."*

INSIGHTS
Question or Focus (if any)

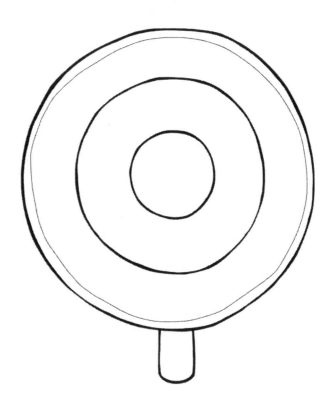

Practice 79:
READ FOR THE FOUR AGREEMENTS

Written by don Miguel Ruiz with a mind toward ancient Toltec wisdom, each merit their own reading.

The Four Agreements offer a spiritual code of conduct to live without suffering and live a more joyful life. You may combine elements of these exercises to form your own template:

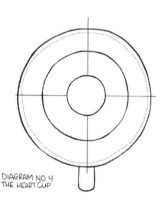

DIAGRAM NO. 4
THE HEART CUP

Be impeccable with your word

Bottom: What your impeccable word has – or has not – looked like to you in the past
Handle: Your role in using your language with clarity and sincerity
Across: Anything you need to know about communicating and thinking in a way that cannot be questioned
Middle: How you can work now on being impeccable with your word
Rim: Future gifts from working on this lesson throughout your life

Always do your best

Bottom: What doing your best has – or has not – looked like to you in the past
Handle: Your role in doing your best
Across: The gifts or people and other living beings that need to benefit from you doing your best
Middle: How you are doing your best now
Rim: The possible outcomes of doing your best in your near future

Don't make assumptions

Bottom: One assumption you have made about yourself (or a person or place that who is distinctly on your mind) that has caused difficulty for you
Handle: Your role in having this assumption
Across: The effect of this assumption
Middle: How you might be making assumptions about this situation now
Rim: How to let go of making this assumption and others like it

Don't take anything personally

Bottom: One time you have taken something personally that has caused difficulty for you
Handle: Your role in taking it personally
Across: The effect this has had for you
Middle: How you might be taking things personally about this situation now
Rim: How to forgive and move on from taking things such as this personally in your near future

Unfold this reading: Divide your cup in four parts and assign each one to one of the four agreements.

INSIGHTS
Question or Focus (if any)

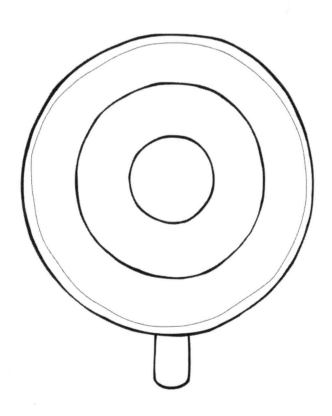

OTHER CREATIVE DIVINATION PRACTICES

1) Draw a tarot or oracle card or rune, etc. to determine the direction or framework for your tea leaf reading before you begin.

2) Storytelling

Look for:
- a talisman or other special object (it could save your adventurer or it could be the cause of a curse they need to break)
- a hero or heroine
- a villain or other obstacle
- a setting or landscape

3) Stars and Significant Dates

Let astrological or historical events guide the theme of your reading or inspire something you would like to discover in your tea cup.

4) Ekphrasis

Liberal arts can provide fresh ways to perceive ourselves – mind, body, heart, and soul. Let a song or album, play or other performance, book or other media, or piece of visual art lead you into a tea leaf reading.

Maybe a painting or type of music helps you find a meditative mindset. Or makes you feel certain emotions. Start there.

Let the tea leaves deepen the conversation of your soul.

A FEW LAST WORDS

Accepting the Mystery

I will always believe in tea leaf readings. In the past, I had convinced myself that divination was only a touch mystical and spiritual. Quick to excuse my love for and use of tarot, and later, tea leaf reading, I insisted on finding ways to highlight its logic. For many who engage in divination work, there is an obstacle of stigma. For me, this included guilt and concern that my actions and counsel were harmful or frivolous.

In the early years of studying tarot and tea leaf readings, I learned to appease popular opinions. Divination, I'd say as I jumped to defend my interest in it, is heavy on psychology and the ability to read people. I still agree with skeptics, too, that a persuasive personality assists in transforming a good reader into a great one. I won't discount such ideas, ever. But I also am grateful to the time invested in giving divination – and myself – a true chance. I hope this book helps you do so, too.

Tea leaves can provide believable, worthwhile experiences. They can reveal someone's character and their likely future. It's the pattern principle: The images found in tea leaves convey patterns that can indicate details. People and situations.

I have had countless experiences where my

interpretations have been regarded as accurate. Recently, a first-time client told me my remarks were almost verbatim as one of the most highly regarded psychics in the area, who used a different tool for her readings than I did. Our readings were only days apart.

The Spellwork of Tea Leaves

When we look for answers in a teacup, we may find little miracles. Answers may be simple or intricate. They might resonate immediately. They might heal. They might bring laughter or make no sense at all.

Personal code development is the magickal spellwork that brings perception and metaphor to life. This gives breath to visionaries of all stripes, whether you consider yourself a creative or a diviner or a psychic or a combination of types.

Static definitions for symbols don't get anyone very far, in my experience. Universal symbols deserve respect, but there is enough written about them to fill libraries. Tea leaf reading is the perfect place to start showcasing the possibilities of personal codes.

When I interact with another person over their cup of tea leaves, our eyes may or may not see the same thing. Or I spot a pop culture reference, like Mario jumping towards a block above his head, his arm raised above him. Either way, the experience is an ice breaker. Clients may have sat down expecting an obscure few minutes, and instead we often interact. We create a dialog that unfolds around their values and sense of perception.

Create your Fate

Learning to do readings interests different people for different reasons. A lot of us are drawn to divination because of its aesthetic and because it offers a medium for helping others and sharing advice. Both tarot and tea leaf reading give me something to give back to the world: Both feed my inner poet and occupy my rescuer archetype – Like creative types, many diviners cherish beautiful objects and want to leave the world more beautiful.

Working as a professional reader gives the networker in me reason to interact on social media and in person, and it opens the door to people and functions I would never have imagined. It's been my fortune to read or teach tea leaves at charity events, for a flowmotion festival in a holler in Kentucky, and at places like Goddess Isis Books & Gifts in Englewood, Colorado.

Reading tea leaves has led me to more than what, at first blush, may have seemed delightful, niche events: One of my favorite regular appearances is the Winter Wizarding Waltz. I participated in it my first winter in Lexington, Kentucky, after I moved from Denver, Colorado. It solidified my sense of place and the joy I felt marked a touchstone in my life. 2018 marks my third year as the tea leaf reader for the waltz, a fundraiser for the local branch of the Harry Potter Alliance. Fulfilling a longtime goal, I dressed as Professor Trelawney, J.K. Rowling's professor of divination.

Onward and Upward

Alone, I would've likely never had enough self-motivation to achieve goals and stick to obligations that have unfolded because of a love of divination. Without an interest in returning to the tea leaves, I'd have a lot less opportunity to keep company with unique people.

Divination can aid in tasks large and small. For example, many readers will use a quick reading to help them make a decision, personal or professional. Or they may wish to set their intentions for a particular goal or time period. It is common practice to incorporate divination tools in a myriad of methods.

As for longer term goals or bigger dreams, divination is a powerful tool. Needing visibility as a diviner encourages companionship and cooperation: While developing my tarot and tea leaf reading business, North Star Muse, I have invented social media events with fellow readers, written a guest blog for another tarot professional, and co-created a casting board for divining with charms in honor of poetry month.

Divination has a place, too, in academia. It was a graduate degree that led me back to tarot, several years after setting it aside. When I began my masters at Colorado State University, I wanted a theme for the book-length collection of poetry for the required thesis. After both birds and fairy tales felt too forced, I eagerly dug out my tarot deck and used it for inspiration. That work brought me to a pop culture conference, where I shared some of my tarot poetry and spoke about the writing process and psychology of using the cards as creative fodder.

Soon I wanted to work as a tarot reader. There was no shortage of fairs and helpful, knowledgeable diviners and psychics to support my goal in Denver, Colorado. But boasting a unique talent in addition to fluency in card-slinging became key in keeping my dreams afloat.

Nourish your Intuition

My first exposure to tea leaf reading was when I was a young girl at a favorite Chinese restaurant in Grand Junction, Colorado, where I grew up. My grandmother liked to order tea with some of our meals and told little stories as she looked inside the bottom of each teapot.

She did it only a few times, but it later inspired me

– gave me permission, that is – to do "my own thing" and develop into a tea leaf reader.

My grandmother read the leaves in a spirit of playfulness that I feel I use in my own divination: The first tea leaf reading I did was very impromptu, for a friend almost ten years ago. I didn't know what to expect, but simply believed I could do it – I'd been reading tarot for maybe a dozen years at that point, so why not? After almost deciding the abundance of leaves didn't yield any special insight, one image struck me – a large bow, like *Cat in the Hat* wears.

Finally, an interpretation was fluid and immediate. This big bow meant my friend needed to treat love with joy – to let her relationship move easily and to show it off. But to make sure it is well-centered. Focused. Tied well.

My grandmother and I never sat down to practice tea readings together. But the first tea reading I did nourished me and I returned for more, perhaps after a couple years. I bought Caroline Dow's *Tea Leaf Reading for Beginners: Your Fortune in a Cup* and the tea leaf fortune cards book and deck by Rae Hepburn. Both continue to help me interpret the unexpected, whether it comes to tea cups, clouds, visits from birds and other animals, or shapes made by jams and crackers and cheeses as I pair them at my day job as a cheese specialist.

I will always believe the real magick of performing readings is this: The act of divination and many of those who pursue it have my respect. Studying and examining and writing about tarot and tea leaf readings have been one of the most generative, life-saving experiences I have ever had. It has made me a better human being. It has always connected me to those around me. It has given me a wealth of laughter, surprises, and comfort.

As I grow into it, creative divination is my logical and mystical home.

LIST OF PRACTICES

PART TWO: Reading As

ABOUT THE AUTHOR

Creative diviner Tabitha Dial uses tarot, tea leaves, and poetry to develop her personal code, and hopes you cherish your methods, too. She interprets tea leaves while cosplaying as Professor Trelawney to benefit Lexpecto Patronum, Lexington, Kentucky's Harry Potter Alliance. Poetry written for her Masters in Fine Arts from Colorado State University has appeared in *Arcana: The Tarot Poetry Anthology*, and in *Tarot in Culture, Volume Two*.

Her articles on SpiralNature.com include how to write tarot poetry, how to create tarot-inspired wreaths, how to use tarot to uncover your shadow side, and more.

Tabitha enjoys sharing her experience at tea leaf reading parties and by doing private tarot and tea leaf readings. Her services are also available for public events. Tabitha teaches tea leaf reading, tarot haiku, and other workshops for writers.

Tabitha's shop of tarot and tea readings and more of her reflections on divination can be found at NorthStarMuse.com. You can also drop her a line at tabithadial@gmail.com.

Made in the USA
Middletown, DE
25 June 2023

33511011R00144